4-24-01

THIS MOTHER'S DAUGHTER

By Nelvia M. Brady

Copyright©1999, Nelvia M. Brady.

First Edition

Published by Nelvia M. Brady
This Mother's Daughter
47 W. Polk Street
PMB 100-141
Chicago, Illinois 60605

Printed in the United States of America

Cover design by Ophelia M. Chambliss

ISBN:0-9673751-0-X   Hardcover
ISBN:0-9673751-2-6   Paperback

Library of Congress Cataloging-in-Publication Data
Brady, Nelvia M.
    This Mother's Daughter / Nelvia M. Brady
99-98100 CIP

Visit our website:
www.thismothersdaughter.com

*E*very mother's daughter is of

a new generation and with each passing year,

those daughters become women and take their place in a

society with slowly evolving changes in lifestyles.

Those changes necessitate maintaining pride and dignity

as a female as well as a belief in a loving humanity. May we all

rise to the occasion of preparing a better world for ourselves and

our children.

—NANCY WILSON, 1976

THIS MOTHER'S DAUGHTER (LYRICS)

Wise beyond her years, This Mother's Daughter is gonna bring tears
Tears to her family
Tears to the men who hold her tenderly

This Mother's Daughter will ride the wind
This Mother's Daughter will see the end of time go by
With time to cry oo oo oo

Wise beyond her days This Mother's Daughter is gonna make waves
Waves like the stormy sea
Storms in the men who want her desperately

This Mother's Daughter will ride the wind
This Mother's Daughter will see the end of time go by
With time to cry oo oo oo

Wise beyond the rain, This Mother's Daughter is gonna know pain
Pain in her heart and soul
Pain in the eyes of men she will control

This Mother's Daughter will ride the wind
This Mother's Daughter will see the end of time go by
With time to cry oo oo oo

Music and Lyrics by
Eugene McDaniels
Copyright 1973
Skyforest Music, Inc.
Recorded by Nancy Wilson
Capitol Records, 1976

Contents

Daughters Share their Stories

Daughters Share Mother's Wisdom

DEDICATION

This book was written in honor of Mother's Day 2000 and is lovingly dedicated to my nieces Danielle, Andrea, Nelvia, Desirèe, Jessica, Davena, Brittani, Bria and Janel, and all of the African-American Mothers and daughters of the new millennium.

ACKNOWLEDGEMENTS

This Mother's Daughter could not have been written without the direction and guidance of the Spirit. First and foremost, I must acknowledge the divine direction I received from God which is best captured in the scripture, Proverbs 3:5&6: Trust in the Lord with all thine heart; and lean not unto thine own understanding. In all thy ways acknowledge him and he will direct your path.

This Mother's Daughter is the combined effort of hundreds of African-American Mothers and daughters who responded to my request for their input. I corresponded with these women via e-mail and the Internet. I also distributed and received postcards to gather information about the "simple wisdom" that daughters had learned from their Mothers. The names of many of these women are listed in the contributors section. I sincerely appreciate the extraordinary and overwhelming response.

I owe my heartfelt thanks to the twenty daughters whose stories are told in *This Mother's Daughter*. They gave their time and shared their stories in lengthy one-on-one interviews. We shared laughter, as well as tears, as we talked about their Mother/daughter relationships. I thank them for their honesty, confidence, and most of all for sharing themselves and their Mothers' wisdom.

Special thanks are extended to Raynard Hall, a master of e-mail among African-Americans and to Michele Kendall, for managing the compilation and input of hundreds of responses. My profound thanks and appreciation are due to Gloria Howard, who toiled long hours transcribing the interviews, typing the manuscript and contributing in every way to insure that I met my tight timetable. She came through every time and never let me down.

Thanks are expressed to my Midwife, Niambi Jaha, for her support, and for keeping me on track as I prepared for the birth of *This Mother's Daughter*. Joyce Owens Anderson was phenomenal in the identification of the Artists whose art was considered for the cover of *This Mother's Daughter*. I am sincerely grateful to Tina Jenkins Bell for her editorial guidance.

I am greatly indebted to William Cox of *Black Issues Book Review* and Jeff Wright of Urban Ministries, Inc., for their sage advice to a newcomer to the publishing world. Through their referrals, I received encouragement and guidance from Adrienne Ingrum, Marilyn Allen and other critical players in the publishing industry.

Special thanks are due to my Pastor and his wife, Rev. Jeremiah Wright and Mrs. Ramah Wright, for their early endorsement of this effort and for extending the support of my church family, Trinity United Church of Christ.

True appreciation is extended to all of this "child's" aunts and uncles including Anthony, Daisy, Brenda, and Jacqueline. My thanks are due to Uncle Allen for feeding my Spirit whenever I needed it. A special expression of appreciation is extended to Aunt Marian whose quiet and steadfast support, helped nurture this pregnancy to full term. I am grateful to many others who came to my aid or challenged my thinking in ways that eased the birth of this book, including Godparents Willie, Wynona, Rachel and T. J.

I owe deep gratitude, sincere thanks and love to Bill, who nurtured and loved me and my unborn "child," throughout the pregnancy that gives birth to *This Mother's Daughter*. Bill gave vision when I lacked it, encouragement when I doubted, strength when I weakened, and most of all shared his unconditional love, always. His support is deeply woven into every single line of this book. To Bill, I am eternally grateful.

Finally, I extend my love and my appreciation for my life and existence to my Mother, Jessie Pearl. She is the primary contributor and inspiration for this book. My everlasting love and heartfelt thanks are due to her. It is because of Jessie Pearl that I am *This Mother's Daughter*.

INTRODUCTION

Jessie Pearl is my Mother and I am *This Mother's Daughter*. Jessie Pearl has been the most significant person to prepare me and my four sisters, as African-American women to enter the new millennium. Preparing African-American daughters for life is a serious matter. We live in a world where daughters in general are undervalued and where African-American daughters are even more challenged to maintain personal and family pride, dignity and a belief in a loving humanity amidst racism and sexism. Our lives, like time, are on a continuum of critical developmental changes, experiences and emotions. Many of us go through these changes, experiences and emotions with wisdom, guidance and strong assistance provided primarily by the Mothers and Mother Figures in our lives. Our Mothers are our first teachers, and our education from them and connection to them begins, quite literally, while we are still in their wombs.

Our Mothers provide for us a voice of wisdom that is too seldom acknowledged even by those daughters who reap the awesome, yet sometimes unanticipated benefits. It is the wisdom of African-American Mothers that connects us to each other as women and as daughters.

What do I mean when I speak of the wisdom of African-American Mothers? First, for me, this wisdom encompasses the good, practical judgment or common sense we are taught both directly through our Mother's words and actions, as well as indirectly through what they do not say and do during our lives. To attain this wisdom we, as daughters, must learn. We must use our capacity to gain the knowledge and information that our Mothers and Mother Figures have available for our use.

We speak of the Wisdom of Jesus and the Wisdom of Solomon. We speak of the wisdom of our ancestors, our elders, our leaders, our pastors, our grandmothers, and we speak of the wisdom of our Mothers. The experiences in our lives that yield this wisdom are not always the experiences that we reflect upon fondly. Wisdom, though exalted in character as an outcome, is many times attained through conflict, turmoil, and hardship. Our lessons are sometimes delivered to us even in spite of ourselves and in ways that we seldom understand until we find ourselves delivering that very same wisdom to other daughters.

When we have the occasion to reflect upon our lives, we often find ourselves sounding like our Mothers and doing the very same things that they did. Certainly, we never dreamed we'd see ourselves doing and saying things their way. As a matter of fact, we promised ourselves that we would never do it their way. We find ourselves wishing we'd listened, or even saying, "I wish she had told me that." Much of the practical insight that African-American Mothers have attempted to pass on is being lost. In our technology-driven society, there is a need to move quickly and skip steps. Mothers are busy earning a living and are teaching daughters poorly developed life skills that are not based in sound wisdom and healthy experiences. Mothers, in many of our communities, are so young that they have had little chance to experience life, before they are positioned to ready daughters for this complex world. Grandmothers, other extended family members, and Mother Figures may not be geographically close enough to help. Even those of us fortunate enough to have Mothers and Mother Figures willing and able to pass on their wisdom, didn't or don't pay attention, didn't or don't understand, or considered it outdated, and cliché.

We have sought help in so many places. We have turned to a plethora of self-help books and classes on how to live life, find happiness and be a good Mother or daughter. We have sought wisdom from celebrity Mothers and daughters, talk show hosts, psychics, astrologers, and advice columnists. We have turned to drugs, alcohol and other abusive behavior when we've not been able to manage our lives. Nowhere have we told our own real life stories and stepped back collectively to see what we have really learned from our Mothers. As African-American Mothers and daughters, we can neither hope nor expect others to listen to us until we first acknowledge and listen to each other. That is why I wrote *This Mother's Daughter*.

This Mother's Daughter is not a scholarly treatise on Mothers, nor a psychological analysis of our Mother's impact on our growth and development. It is a simple work that shares the stories, experiences and simple truths of African-American daughters learned from their Mothers. These daughters are not fictitious. They are real. They are housewives and housekeepers, evangelists and ministers, nurses and physicians, clerks and executives, AFDC and Ph.D. They are from Africa and Alabama and from New York and North Carolina. They are all ages. They are your friends, coworkers, neighbors, relatives and acquaintances. They are daughters from all walks of life that have birthed and raised daughters to positions in all walks of life. *This Mother's Daughter* is intended to bring to the forefront stories that share the wisdom and messages given to daughters from the hearts of our African-American Mothers.

Though this book had been on my mind and in my heart for many years, in order to finally move to write *This Mother's Daughter*, I had to undergo a personal transformation. I believe that is why the Spirit entered my life in such a profound, direct and timely manner. Messages that this book needed to be written began to come from everywhere. Events, support and people began coming to me that could have only been called into my life by the Spirit. The Spirit was necessary so that this effort would not be censored and so that I would be required to rely on my heart and those spiritual messages as my guides in developing this work.

The Spirit worked quickly and directly, causing me to see clearly that this book was not about me, but was something much bigger that needed to be shared broadly. As a result of the Spirit's intervention, I found myself pregnant with *This Mother's Daughter*. At fifty-one years old, with no husband or previous pregnancies, my miracle "child" was conceived on the evening of April 9, 1999. Coincidentally, this was the day, proclaimed nationally as the best day for conception to occur to birth a millennium day baby.

There was never the thought of aborting this "child." At my age, it was clear that this pregnancy was a gift and a miracle. I also knew that a purpose was to be served by the birth and nurturing of this "child."

As I readied myself for the birth of my "child," I needed support and input from others who knew about being a Mother and a daughter. I sought information from everywhere and hundreds of African-American Mothers and daughters responded. I asked African-American Mothers and daughters to share with me those short, simple, pieces of advice, pearls of wisdom and lessons for life that Mothers or Mother Figures had shared and passed on. We've all heard these things. We remember and repeat them and we laugh together as Sisters about such things as " keep your dress down and your panties up."

As I gathered this "simple wisdom," it became clear that my "fetus" was maturing and I needed to know more. I sought out other African-American Mothers and daughters and asked them to tell me the whole story of their relationship with their Mother. I wanted to know, about the simple and complex lessons that daughters learn from the Mother or Mother Figure in their lives. These African-American Mothers and daughters were eager to talk, and they freely shared their most intimate Mother and daughter feelings and experiences.

Through *This Mother's Daughter*, I hope to share that wisdom we glean from the needs, hopes and wishes of our Mothers and the unique relationships we share. In these pages, daughters will tell you about their experiences with their Mother or Mother Figure whether their experiences are rewarding or troubling. Their stories express intense devotion as well as unveil psychic scars. They move from early childhood, to growing older and facing the mortality of the women they call Mother, Mama, Mom, Momma, Big Mama or Ma'Dear.

You will read about how childhood experiences with our Mothers shape our lives and how difficult it is to shed experiences that negatively affect our functioning. You will observe time and time again, how daughters are seldom openly informed about their development as women, about menstruation, and sexuality. You will remember how we fill in these blanks with talk from peers and with experimentation. You will be amazed at how frequently Mothers and daughters became pregnant following their very first sexual experience, when they know little about themselves, not to mention their bodies. You will wonder why, as Mothers and daughters, we rarely talk about "what to do" and how often we talk about "what not to do" in our relationships, especially in our love relationships. You will note the generational differences in our attitudes about sex and love. You will worry about your own future and that of your Mother when you read of Mothers who are elderly and in need of care from daughters. You will consider how your relationship with your Mother has impacted how you relate to your daughter, how you relate to men, how you relate to other women, and how you view life in general. You will chuckle when you hear what Mothers tell their daughters about money, friendship, personal hygiene, dating and beauty. You will shed tears about the struggles African-American Mothers and daughters face with sexual abuse and relationship violence, and other burdens they quietly carry. You will take pride in their heroism and acknowledge the strength, resiliency and courage they have shown against great odds. Finally, and most importantly, you will feel the durability of the bond and the power of the love that flows between each of the women of *This Mother's Daughter*.

This Mother's Daughter can serve as a tool to create discussion with your Mother or daughter and to reclaim your Mother/daughter story. Believe me when I say that it will change the course of your conversation as it changed mine with my Mother. Use this book to talk with younger African-American Mothers and daughters to give back and pass on our collective, extraordinary, and timeless wisdom. Use this book to learn and to help yourself as you journey through this life and face the challenges emanating from a world unfriendly to us. Use *This Mother's Daughter* as a way to help heal, to be of service, and most importantly, to transmit unconditional love.

DAUGHTERS SHARE
THEIR STORIES

Erica and Rose

During our lives, it is our relationships that provide some of the most significant lessons, the most cherished experiences, and the greatest sources of opportunity for personal growth and development. When there is love, the potential for personal growth is greatly enhanced. Outside of our spiritual relationship, there is none that offers more potential for positive growth than a loving relationship between daughter and mother. Erica and her mother Rose love each other dearly and are always there for one another. Whatever Erica has encountered in life she has always known that Rose would be there for her. Erica proudly returns Rose's legacy of love. She knows that she is a good daughter because Rose gave her love as a family dowry.

ERICA AND ROSE

The first thing that catches the eye when one sees Erica, and her mother, Rose is that both have such beautiful, perfectly coifed salt and pepper hair. They are also fashionably and impeccably attired. Both have warm, outgoing personalities, cheerful dispositions, sharp wits, and a secure, confident presence. They are genetically, physically, and emotionally bonded as daughter and mother.

Erica is fifty-one years old and lives in the east. She is an attorney by training, but once was a dancer and she still has strong, shapely dancer's legs and a firm girlish figure. She is now an entrepreneur and is the first child and only daughter of the two children born to Rose. Rose, raised in Tennessee, is also an only daughter, born to Katie. She seems far too energetic and moves so quickly that one would not believe that she is in her seventies. She has been happily married to Erica's father for more than fifty years and worked most of her life on the night shift in an electrical factory.

"BIRDS OF A FEATHER, FLOCK TOGETHER"

Erica was reared in a family where both parents worked full-time. Rose chose to work the night shift so that she would be available to raise her daughter during the day. After working all night, she would come home and provide

2

Erica with a strong mother figure and with all of the advantages that any full-time homemaker would provide for her children. Rose had been raised very strictly and sometimes had to be cautioned by her husband that childrearing practices that were good for her, were not necessarily good for Erica. She needed and desired this balance to assure that Erica would be raised in a manner appropriate to the times, and in an environment conducive to becoming a well-rounded and secure woman.

Erica recalls a very happy, carefree childhood and a beautiful mother/daughter relationship with Rose. Her mother's home had been the gathering place for her friends and other children. Erica thought that this was rather special, in that everyone loved her mother and viewed her home as the nucleus of fun, activity, and love. Even when Erica was not socializing with other children at home, Rose was always around Erica and her friends. Rose involved herself in all aspects of Erica's upbringing. She chaperoned parties, chauffeured Erica and her friends to events, took them shopping, and seemed to always be in close proximity. Though in a stricter overall environment, this was the very same way Rose had been raised.

I was always in clubs and I was always the president. Most of the activities were at my house like sleepovers, parties. She always cooked and there was always food. Most of the fun things that people remember about growing up were happening at my house. Now I realize it was great for her because she knew exactly what I was doing. I always joke with her because although she only had two kids, she probably always had a huge grocery bill. Everyone came to my house and ate. I was the one that if the party ended at ten she was picking me up at nine thirty, screaming my name out in the basement, turning on the lights and all that. She was that kind of mother. Everybody knew it. I just thought that was the way all mothers were.

"ANYTHING WORTH DOING IS WORTH DOING RIGHT"

Erica remembers her childhood fondly and is proud of the fact that a strong, loving African-American woman raised her. She not only was the beneficiary of Rose's strengths, but also those of her grandmother, Katie, who often took care of her in Rose's absence. Erica internalized several messages that Rose delivered during her childhood. They center on cleanliness in the home and personal hygiene; work and money; and education.

My mother is a fanatic about cleaning. I mean you were in fresh underwear, your slip couldn't be dirty and you washed clothes. Saturday was a big cleaning day. The way I was raised, when you washed dishes it meant you washed all the dishes and you dried all the dishes. But you also had to wash the stove, wash the refrigerator and sweep. That was all a part of it. When she'd come home at night if it weren't done, you had to get up and do whatever you didn't do. You never left the dishes in the sink. She said dishes didn't dry overnight. Her kitchen was always spotless at night because those were the rules. I told her when I got older, that I really hated that about her. But now, when I clean the house I know how to turn the mattress, to get in the corners, do the closet and all that old-fashioned cleaning. I know how to do that because I learned that at an early age.

"IN A MARRIAGE MAKE SURE THAT YOU ALWAYS HAVE OUR MONEY AND YOUR MONEY"

The second critical message of wisdom that Rose delivered to Erica centered on work and money. In Rose's eyes, work was important for women. Employment provided a sense of independence and security that was important to Rose. Though her marriage was happy and secure, she always considered the possibility that she would need to be prepared to take care of herself and her children alone. Work was the vehicle that provided this security. Additionally, Rose's mother impressed upon her the need for women to have their own resources, separate and secret from the men in their lives. Rose passed this belief along to Erica. Erica is sometimes amused that Rose maintains her "stash," her "get away cash," but that's what Rose had learned from her mother a generation before.

I think that was one of the first messages my mother delivered to me. It was important that you work. If you worked, then you were not totally dependent on your husband for anything. That gave you a certain amount of freedom. That was always important, an independence. My mother always worked, and I never thought it was unusual. My mother has also always said save, save, save. She is obsessed with saving, and she's made me obsessed. She says that you should always have your own stash and have your money. The last couple of years she's been keeping hers in these different places. Whenever I go home, she says, "Erica, this is my stash." I say, Ma look, I can't remember if you keep changing places. You can't remember either, so let's just put this money in one place." I was home recently, and she pulled out a Mason jar and it actually had cash with a little note hidden in her closet. My grandmother had money like that too.

4

"USE YOUR HEAD FOR SOMETHING
MORE THAN JUST A HAT RACK"

Erica always understood how hard Rose worked in the factory and also knew that she had not completed college. Rose was determined that her daughter would get a college education and her third message to Erica was that college was a must-do. There was no question that Erica would get an education because Rose did not want her daughter to have to work in a factory.

She always thought that education was important. I was going to college. I never had a memory of not planning on going to college. I went to grammar school, high school, and there was no question—I was going to college. She valued education as a way to be independent, and also because she worked in a factory, she wanted me to have a degree. I would have been the first one, on both sides of my family to get a college degree. That was very important to her.

"WHY BUY THE COW IF YOU CAN GET THE MILK FREE"

As Erica reached puberty and the beginning stages of womanhood, Rose continued to be open and forthright. Rose also paid close attention to issues of personal hygiene. Though Rose urged Erica to be especially clean during her menstrual, she warned Erica not to take baths or wash her hair.

I said this doesn't make any sense because you'll stink. So then we sat and had some conversations about it. She explained that this was a natural part of being a woman. Don't be afraid of it. But you know you have to be really clear about keeping clean.

Being pregnant, in my mother's mind, would have just been the worst thing. She thought that would impede your life and education. If you got pregnant, you couldn't go to college. Then you had to work in a factory. If you worked in a factory, you couldn't have all the others things in life. Her message was always a real practical message as opposed to a moral message.

Though Erica had been a cheerleader and was very popular in high school, she was not really considered very attractive by boys. She didn't have a history of being pursued, had not dated very much, and was generally quite inexperienced. This was the circumstance when she decided to become sexually active.

I was so disappointed in the whole experience. I had read a lot of books and I was expecting the bells to ring and the sky to light up. It was just real painful and it was really just unpleasant. I think I did it because I felt you couldn't be a virgin going to college. I just did it.

"DON'T FALL IN LOVE WITH NO MAN'S POTENTIAL"

Fortunately, Erica did not get pregnant. She did, however, fall in love and decided to get married at the end of her freshman year in college. Not only was she in love, but she had the mistaken notion that once married, the sex automatically got better.

Rose was, of course, not pleased with Erica's decision to marry. She was actually quite appalled. Initially, Rose thought that Erica wanted to marry because she was pregnant. That not being the case, Rose was even more concerned that Erica would jeopardize her education and her future in the name of love. Rose told Erica she couldn't get married and threatened to cut off support. Rose complained that Erica had nothing in common with the man and that she'd get pregnant, wouldn't complete college, and all of the other admonitions that she felt were warranted. However, this was Erica's first real boyfriend. He was attentive, and he was receptive to her nurturing qualities. Most importantly, she was in love. Against Rose's wishes, Erica married.

Rose's marriage, in Erica's eyes, had been a beautiful, loving, and happy relationship. She had never heard her parents even curse at one another, and certainly there was never anything physical between them. They never argued about money. They made decisions together and shared similar interests. There were no role definitions or distinctions based on gender. They loved each other. Erica quickly realized that her parents' relationship and marriage was not to be hers. She realized early in her marriage that her husband was not a hard worker, nor was he a good communicator. Her marital relationship was nothing like the one she knew best. As Rose had predicted, Erica dropped out of college for a while and later returned to junior college. It took her six years to complete her undergraduate degree. Rose stuck by Erica, used her "stash" to help her financially, and insisted that Erica continue her studies. Meanwhile, Erica began to experience abuse and infidelity in her marriage. She came to the realization that she was terribly unhappy, but she was also determined to try to make things work, if only to prove that Rose was wrong in her prediction of the negative direction her marriage would take.

I dropped out of school and I worked a year. My mother sent me money and kept saying, "You've got to go back to school." Were it not for her, I probably would've given up and just tried to support him. But I listened to her. I went back to school. It was her insistence that kept me in school.

The summer before graduation and after four years of marriage, Erica's husband moved out. She did not know how to tell Rose. When her parents and other family members arrived for the graduation ceremonies, there was no husband.

The only place I could talk to them privately, because all of my relatives were there, was in the bathroom. So I pulled them in the bathroom and I said, mommy and daddy, I have something to tell you. My mother said, "Oh no, you're not going to graduate." I said, Oh, no, that's not it. My father said, "What is it?" I said, we have split up. My father said, "Is that all, okay, let's go graduate." We never missed a beat.

Erica had learned from Rose that love was an emotion that had to be backed up by action. She had come from a household where Rose was pampered, where marriage was a partnership, and love was demonstrated in behaviors, not simply in words. She had experienced just the opposite in her own marriage.

My mother was not a romantic. Love was a person who, like my father, always brought his money home, took care of his family, supported you. She always felt love was an act of partnership more so than a romantic concept. My evidence of what love is was in my parent's relationship. That's what I was looking for in marriage. I'm not sure if I'll ever find it like that.

Soon after her divorce Erica remarried and has now been married for more than twenty-five years. She never had any children, but has been instrumental in raising several of her husband's relatives. Rose has talked to Erica about growing older, and has prepared her well for the changes that she will face as a woman. She proudly wears her hair in its natural gray, and like Rose, refuses to take hormones. Erica has reflected on her life, and sees now that many of the things that Rose tried to teach her about life are becoming her reality. She now knows how important it is to have a mate who shares similar values. She appreciates the importance of being independent and believes that good relationships require sacrifice as well as commitment.

It's been a real struggle to try to match what I've grown up with to my reality. My current husband is very close to my parents and he's trying to emulate some of the

1

things that he sees. I think that you really need someone that has a common value system with you: how you grew up, what your parents were like; and the kind of indoctrination, and the issues that you had. I think that when marriages get in trouble, those are the things you go back to. I haven't been successful in choosing someone that has enough of that. This is my second marriage; it's been a lot of work. Sometimes I wonder if it was a mistake being married my whole life. I would like the experience of being single, taking care of myself, making my own decisions, being totally responsible or irresponsible, as the case may be. Sometimes I wonder if that was an experience that I should have had.

Erica truly values Rose as a mother and as a friend. As she grows older, their relationship becomes stronger and stronger. They travel together, shop worldwide, attend social functions, and even though they live in different cities, Erica has only missed spending one Christmas at home.

I feel real blessed. You can take my mother anyplace. You want to hang all night, she can hang. She can play cards. She's hilarious. She talks to everybody. She has taught me a lot. I know now that you have to love yourself first and feel good about yourself before you can bring that to someone else. Most of us look for that in someone else and don't love ourselves enough first. That's the message that I tell young girls all the time. It is very important that you feel good about yourself, your issues, and the things that you want in life. Bring that to relationships. Lay it on the table early.

As I've gotten older, I realize that she was real practical. She was right with that mother wit that she has. Very few things have been wrong. She's honest and she's been an incredible mother. You can tell her anything. She listens. She's not judgmental. She tries to understand, then gives you an opinion. I try to do everything I can for her while she's alive. I've been a damn good daughter and I know that. But loosing her terrifies me.

Anna and Earline

Struggle can be a growth experience. But while we are in a struggle, we can not see its potential to benefit our development. How we experience the struggle and how we meet the challenges that these struggles place before us are of critical importance. Learn from the struggle, grow from it, and then let it go. Childhood was a struggle for Anna who was raised by a foster mother, Earline. Earline constantly berated Anna, regularly threatened her with abandonment and told her that she was ugly. But Anna gained strength and determination from her struggles and came through her stormy life with the unyielding will to survive.

Anna and Earline

Anna is forty-five years old, and at only five feet three inches tall, she struggles with being overweight. She has coffee with cream-colored skin and sleepy, bedroom eyes. She is dressed in a loosely fitting outfit carefully selected to distract from her middle age spread. Anna is an administrative assistant for an association. She has two daughters, Kiya and Rena, and three young grandchildren. Her biological mother is Sonya, who is from Tennessee. Anna is the second daughter of five. However, growing up in the foster care system, Anna speaks of eight different women she has known as mother. Of these women, Earline was the one who most impacted Anna's life and development, and the one she referred to as mother for the longest period of time. Earline was a housewife who had experienced seven unsuccessful pregnancies before taking Anna and her sisters into her care.

Anna lived in foster care homes until she was fifteen years old. Ten of those years were spent in the home of Earline and her husband. She remembers little about her removal from the home of her biological mother, other than getting dressed that day, and the arrival of the social worker. She also remembers that while with her biological mother, she and her sisters were frequently left home alone at night. She suspects that someone reported this circumstance to the authorities, ultimately leading to the foster care placement with Earline.

Earline was an atypical foster parent. She took responsibility for the care of Anna and her three sisters even though she had never previously had foster children in her home. As might be expected, to suddenly be responsible for four young girls was quite a dramatic change in her life. The family lived in a suburban community, and by the standards of outside observers, they had a decent quality of life. Inside the walls of this seemingly normal household, conditions were quite different.

Anna's childhood, in her view, was unhappy and traumatic. Thirty years later, she recalls vividly experience after experience to validate her claims. Other children in this quiet suburb taunted Anna and provided a constant reminder that she was different, just a foster child whose mother had thrown her away. Although these experiences were painful and humiliating, Earline, is Anna's most poignant memory. Earline constantly reminded Anna that Sonya was a whore and weekly threatened to send her away. Anna lived each day with the shame of being born to such a person, and with the fear and threat of rejection and abandonment. Earline was also unkind and somewhat sneaky and duplicitous in her childrearing practices and strategies for disciplining her children. Anna recalls examples of these instances in quick succession, often laughingly, and undoubtedly feeling some agony.

"A HARD HEAD MAKES A SOFT BEHIND"

One incident in my life that crystallizes my experience of growing up with Earline happened when I was twelve years old. I entered a citywide art contest and I submitted several pictures. I came home one day and Earline was looking really sad. I asked her what was wrong? She said, " It's about the art contest." I got afraid because I thought I had disappointed her and that I didn't win. I started getting nervous. I didn't know how she was going to react. I didn't want to win so much for myself; I wanted her to feel proud. So when I started to cry, she said, "You won." I was in disbelief. It was like wait, I'm confused. I'm really confused now. She said, "You won the scholarship." At that point I couldn't even be happy about it because it was set on a different path. I felt cheated, robbed out of some happiness that I had coming.

That was pretty typical of her and she kept me in confusion. She would say I'm leaving the house and I don't care if Jesus Christ comes to the door, I don't want you to answer the door or the phone. So at one point, the phone rang. It rang so much that I started counting the rings. You know, it rang seventeen times and then they would hang up. Then it would ring twenty-five times and hang up. After awhile, I thought it must be an emergency. Back then, with no answering machines, people would give us four rings to get to the phone and then would hang up. So I picked up the phone on the twenty-seventh ring of one call and I said hello. Earline yelled on the other end, "Didn't I tell you not to answer the phone." So I slammed the phone *down. I got it good later.*

Another time she said that she was leaving the house. She was gone for hours. Finally, when it got dark, after we had exhausted our playing, our conversations turned to her. Do you like mama? I hate her. I don't like her. She's too mean. She's always beating us. Now what we didn't realize was that she never left the house. She hid in the front closet. She stepped out right at that moment and started beating us because she had heard everything we'd said.

"You Can't Judge A Book By Its Cover"

Anna recalls other aspects of her childhood and her relationship with Earline that have had a lasting impact on her even to this day. Earline taught Anna that she was not worthy of things of value. Anna attributes her life long battle with low self-esteem to Earline's parenting. Earline promoted an unnecessary poverty consciousness that caused Anna to deny herself and to never be personally generous or self-indulgent. Anna holds on tightly to money and gets very nervous whenever she spends it on herself. Even though she may have the resources, she is always reluctant to provide quality material items for herself. She attributes this to Earline and what was said and did during that ten-year period she was in her care.

It took awhile to get rid of the self-loathing. This is another legacy that Earline left to me. She used to tell me that I was extremely ugly, and that I looked like a dying cow. Her nickname for me was liverlips. She refused to buy a lot of my school pictures, because my eyes looked like a dying cow's eyes. So when I looked in the mirror, I saw an ugly, homely child. I grew up wearing glasses and I had the dark marks on the bridge of my nose. I always felt really ugly. When somebody would say that I was pretty, I would immediately burst into tears. I don't care where I was; I could not control it. It just seemed so cruel. Why would they say that when I know I'm ugly? Why would they be so mean as to say something that was so untrue? It took me a long time, and sometimes I still see that ugly little girl. Even though I know intellectually that I am not perceived as ugly, I can still look in a mirror and see those same dying cow eyes that Earline saw.

Anna did not learn much about her sexuality from Earline. She was told very little and most of that was positioned in fear and negativism. She was quite naïve believing that she was left in a basket on the stair steps, and that she would get pregnant if she kissed boys. She was taught that if you had large breasts early, and she did, it was because boys were orally stimulating and play-

11

ing with them. When explaining menstruation, Earline convinced her that blood would run uncontrollably out of her body every month. She told her that if she tried to stop it that it would back up through her body and run from her nose.

These horror stories about her development frightened and confused Anna. More confusing and frightening for Anna was her awareness that her foster father was molesting her older sister. The situation had been brought to Earline's attention, but she had failed to address the matter. Though he once tried to kiss Anna, he was never successful in going further. The situation was quite complex. On the one hand, Earline chastised Anna about becoming a woman. On the other hand she seemed to take pleasure in displaying Anna's budding womanness to her foster father.

At one point, I can't remember when. I must have been around twelve when all of this started happening. She accused me of thinking I was grown. She takes me into her bedroom. In front of him, she pulls up my T-shirt and tells him that I think that I'm grown because I'm developing breasts. She takes both of my breasts and starts twisting them. Then she pulls my panties down. I had maybe one little baby pubic hair, just one. She snatched it out. It was like she was serving me up on a platter and then getting mad if he responded.

"There's More Than One Way To Skin A Cat"

Anna was fond of reading romance magazines and loved to read about the blissful, passionate, sexy scenes that never resulted in anything other than sheer delight for the participants. To her dismay, her first sexual experience at fourteen years old was disappointing, painful, and unenjoyable. It also resulted in pregnancy. By this time, Earline had been diagnosed with colon cancer and with her condition deteriorating, Anna was moved to another foster home. Earline died the same year that Anna gave birth to her daughter, Kiya. As if her situation were not complicated enough, Anna was now not only a ward of the state, but a mother as well. The baby's father also denied paternity and at fifteen Anna was a single parent.

When I found out I was pregnant, my caseworker said the options were to put my child up for adoption or in a foster home. She told me about this family that could not have children and really wanted a child. They gave me the spiel about how it would be in my baby's best interest to let her go. I couldn't care for her. I was still in foster care and they had to find another place for me to live. Nobody was going to take me and my daughter. It was already hard enough to place a teenager. After six months, I made up my mind. I placed Kiya up for adoption.

From this point, Anna was placed in several other short-term foster homes and was attempting to pursue the process to become an emancipated minor. Her caseworker informed her that the only way to get out of the foster care system was to get married. Now sixteen and dating a man twenty, Anna got pregnant again, and gave birth to her second daughter, Rena. As her social worker had, perhaps facetiously recommended, Anna married her child's father.

"SEX TAKES, BUT LOVE GIVES FREELY OF THE HEART AND SOUL"

When Anna married, she didn't have a clue about love. She had no notion as to how a woman contributes to building a strong marital relationship. The only thing that Anna wanted from marriage was the option of keeping her child and extricating herself from the foster care system. As a young bride and mother, Anna was frequently abused by her husband. She was often left alone at home for long periods with her child and only a few dimes for emergency telephone calls. Unhappy, and with her two-year-old daughter in tow, Anna ran away from her husband to live with Sonya, her biological mother, in Tennessee. Sonya was unaccustomed to being a mother, not to mention a grandmother. The relationship between the estranged mother and daughter was a struggle. Anna was soon sent to meet for the first time, and then to live with, her biological father. Again, things didn't work for the transient young mother.

Finally, after floating between homes for a couple of years, Anna moved into her own apartment. With this move she began a path to spend the next twenty years in and out of relationships with men ranging from brief encounters to a four-year live-in arrangement. As a young woman, all of Anna's life experiences began to meld. The combined effects of a traumatic childhood, poor self-esteem, unresolved tensions with Sonya, unhealthy experiences with men, the stress of motherhood, and guilt related to her first child's adoption were more than Anna could handle. She began to experience periods of deep clinical depression and suicide attempts. She cannot recall any relationship during her life that she would consider successful, even though her definition is simply one where she can have open, honest dialogue in a monogamous climate.

A good relationship would be one with someone whose faults I could tolerate. To sum it up, a relationship with someone I can love in spite of his faults. You know, accepting those faults that don't violate my bottom line. I have a bottom line I've developed over the years. I can not tolerate infidelity. That will cause me to end the relationship. I kept getting into relationships with men who were emotionally unavailable. It was a pattern. They would not realize that they cared for me until it was too late. Once I was no longer interested, then they'd pursue me aggressively. But at that point, I was already committed to ending the relationship. That happened so many times it's not even funny. Like, oh, here we go again. I remember one thing that Earline used to tell me about relationships. She told me, "You're never going to get a man. He'll always have to watch what he says around you because you're so sensitive. He's going to become tired of trying not to hurt your feelings."

"YOU COME INTO THIS WORLD ALONE AND YOU WILL LEAVE THIS WORLD ALONE"

Anna's memory of Earline's death focuses on her last days after she became afflicted with cancer. Initially, Earline blamed the children for her illness. Perhaps as a side effect of her treatments, she became paranoid and even thought that the children were trying to kill her. She once forced Anna to view her colon and the colostomy bag that she wore. The sight of her colon, raw and pink, makes Anna cringe even now. When Earline was near death, Anna was brought back to see her. She remembers nothing of their final deathbed conversation but remembers vividly what she saw.

She had gone from like three hundred pounds to like ninety pounds. I will never forget. She was lying in her bed propped up on one elbow. She lifted up her thin arm and the watch that she had worn for all those years fell down to her shoulder. She let her hair down and it had gotten incredibly long. I still remember the image of how small she was just leaning on the bed. When she took her hair out of the bun, it cascaded down the side of the bed. I saw this tiny, withered woman underneath all of this hair. Her eyes were huge and she was really gaunt. She must have known that she was dying at that point. Her image is burned into my eye. I don't even know if I was capable of hearing her. I just remember her looking so altered.

"IT'S NOT HOW MANY TIMES YOU FALL DOWN THAT COUNTS IT'S HOW MANY TIMES YOU GET UP"

In spite of Anna's unhappy childhood with Earline, she sees many positive things resulting from her experiences that have shaped the woman she is today. She has spent time in therapy and has done a tremendous amount of reading to improve her self- concept. Anna has reunited with Kiya, is working and living a healthy life as a single woman. She is still seeking a good relationship with a man. The difference is that Anna now loves herself and believes that this point had to be reached before a successful relationship with anyone could be a possible. Her feelings about Earline have mellowed as she has reflected on her life, and as she has matured.

I loved her. I had lived other places before that ten-year span, it felt more stable. I wasn't moving around from place to place, even though I was threatened with it all the time. But yeah, I did love her in a way that you love people that you don't like. She loved me too, in the way that she was capable of. We were fed, we had clothes, we went to church every Sunday, and we were part of a community. For ten years she kept us, so I think she must have loved us. My emotional life was in such turmoil that I felt suicidal for many years and I wanted answers to why my life was so hard? Why was it so horrible? Why did it seem like every time something good was going to happen, something bad would happen? My sweet was always mixed with bitter.

I know that I am a survivor. I know that I have the power to speak on my circumstances and reshape them. Just by being conscious of how I say what I say. I also knew that I would be a late bloomer because I had a lot of issues to sort out. For a long time I didn't think that I was loved at all. I didn't know what the experience of love felt like. I thought because I am not loved, I am therefore unworthy of being loved. I know now that's not true. I know that Earline loved us in the way that she was able to love. Now that I'm older, I know that she was shaped by her experiences as much as I've been shaped by mine.

I tell my daughters that whatever they are currently experiencing is survivable. They can survive it. That's my message to them. It's more about survival than anything else. Fear paralyzes you and keeps you from doing what you think you want to do. But then, if you have a burning passion to do something, you can speak life to it. The events will follow to support doing that. That was a gift from Earline, because for some reason it became imperative to survive. I wasn't concerned about living well; I just wanted to survive.

Kᴇʟʟɪ ᴀɴᴅ Cʜᴀʀʟᴏᴛᴛᴇ

If you have loved someone in the very best way that you know how, then you need not worry about their love for you. They will always hold you close in their hearts. Kelli spent her early life loving her adoptive mother Charlotte and trying to understand why they were so different from one another. Getting to her roots helped her in self-understanding and taught her that she has an infinite capacity to give and that the gift of love has no limits.

Kᴇʟʟɪ ᴀɴᴅ Cʜᴀʀʟᴏᴛᴛᴇ

Kelli is dressed especially glamorous for her birthday party later on the Saturday evening that we meet. She is a twenty-nine-year-old nurse and the mother of a fifteen-month old daughter. She is of average height, and her normally full-figure is still carrying some weight from her pregnancy. She is an attractive young woman with very smooth dark brown skin and long thin cornrowed braids. Her smile lights up the room as we begin our conversation about her adoptive mother Charlotte. Charlotte is a fifty-six-year-old nurse. She and her husband adopted Kelli when she was less than a year old. Later, Charlotte bore a son.

Kelli, originally Darcel, learned very early in her life that she was adopted. However, it was not until she was eight years old that Charlotte decided to explain the circumstances of her birth and subsequent adoption. Her explanation included very little detail and information about Kelli's biological mother. Charlotte was simple and to the point. Kelli was told that her mother was young when she became pregnant and decided to give her up for adoption. Charlotte also attempted to impress upon Kelli that being adopted made her a special child in that she, unlike children being raised by their biological mothers, had been chosen. That was the extent of the conversation.

During childhood, Kelli frequently fantasized about the identity of her natural mother. As an imaginative child, her fantasies were more than whimsical speculations. She imagined that her birth mother was the well-known recording artist, Chaka Khan. In part, Kelli conceived a singer as her make-believe mother because she loved to sing. She also had a wonderful voice. Fantasizing about a mother like Chaka Khan kept her from being angry about being placed for adoption. She rationalized that a woman at such a high level of musical

16

accomplishment and prominence certainly could not manage the burden of a child. How could Chaka Khan be a mother with the heavy demands of her professional life? How could a child fit into the worldwide travel schedule that she maintained? After all, we're talking about the talented and famous Chaka Khan. When Kelli would have disagreements with Charlotte, she would escape to her fantasy mother and seriously retort that she was going to contact Chaka Khan and have her come to get her.

"Always Paddle Your Own Canoe"

Notwithstanding the fact that she was an adopted child, Kelli had what she considered a "normal" childhood. Two areas of her childhood emerge as significant to her overall development. Both areas bear relationship to the fact that she was adopted. First, Kelli always felt that she was quite different from Charlotte in terms of basic personality traits. Kelli was extremely bubbly, full of fun, laughter, and song. She was a natural extrovert. Charlotte, on the other hand, was reserved, subdued, and had little sense of humor. In fact, she would become irritated at Kelli's displays and with her constant tendency to sing no matter what she was doing around the house. Second, Kelli was physically quite different from Charlotte. In her days, Charlotte's dark skin was sometimes viewed negatively, but her keen features were considered beautiful. Much to her consternation, she was often referred to as a "Black China Doll." Kelli, to the contrary, did not meet any of these standards of beauty. Charlotte constantly reminded Kelli that she did not consider her an attractive person and as such, she would need to work harder in life to find security. She drew a correlation between beauty and success as well as with the potential for finding a mate in life. Charlotte related what she considered Kelli's unattractiveness to the critical importance of her receiving a good education. She frequently reminded Kelli that she was "not one of those pretty girls" so she had better get good education.

Charlotte stressed education throughout Kelli's childhood and its importance was frequently tied to the fact that she would have few other alternatives. It was critical to Kelli's future that she be a smart and successful person because she certainly could not expect to marry and have a husband to help support her.   Kelli accepted this theory and modeled herself based on Charlotte's prognosis. She also adopted Charlotte as a professional role model deciding early in her life that she was going to be a nurse. Kelli was successful in completing high school and subsequently with strong support from Charlotte, completed a degree in nursing.

At the age of twenty Kelli beat Charlotte's odds, became engaged, and married. She recalls that on her wedding day her husband-to-be was late arriving to the church. Already the typical nervous bride, Kelli was concerned about his delay. She was worried, concerned for his well-being and uneasy about what might be the reasons behind his late arrival. In the midst of her anxiety, Charlotte provided her interpretation of the reason and also gave Kelli one final dose of self-esteem-diminishing medicine.

When I got married, we were waiting for my fiancé to arrive and she said, "He is not coming. Nobody is gonna marry you, Kelli."

"IT IS NOT SO IMPORTANT WHAT YOU HAVE IN YOUR LIFE BUT WHO YOU HAVE IN YOUR LIFE"

As Kelli grew older, she put aside her Chaka Khan fantasy and began to thoughtfully consider the identity of her biological mother. She would talk about her interest in knowing more, but never took any serious actions. When she reached the legal age of twenty-one years old, it was Charlotte who decided to initiate a search. By this time, the laws had become much more liberal, and adoptive children all over the country were seeking and finding information about their natural parents. Two years later, the telephone call came to Charlotte informing her that Kelli's mother had been located. Initially, Kelli did not know what to do with this information. She was excited, yet she was afraid to take the next step. Charlotte took a neutral position expressing some doubt that anything substantive would develop between the biological mother and Kelli because so much time had passed without contact. Kelli decided to follow through and eventually met her biological mother and her half sister. The meeting was immediately positive and was the beginning of a relationship triangle: adoptive mother-daughter-biological mother. Kelli, to be sure, was positioned smack dead in the middle.

It went from there. When we first talked she said, "I knew you would get in touch with me. I always knew you would." She came out here and we have really developed our relationship to where I'm here tonight celebrating my birthday with her. Initially, Charlotte was supportive, but since then she hasn't been at all. Charlotte wants to talk; she doesn't want to listen. She feels very betrayed. I can't really understand that. I try to tell her all the time; you are always my mother. I'm not gonna kick you to the curb because I found my biological mother. She's not going to take me from you. I feel in a very awkward position. We are all adults and there is enough love.

"The Apple Don't Fall Too Far From The Tree"

Having met her biological mother explains a lot to Kelli about her identity. Her bubbly personality is much like that of her biological mother. Her biological mother is also a singer, though unlike Kelli's fantasy, her name is not Chaka Khan. The physical resemblance is remarkable, with mother and daughter sharing very similar body types and facial features. Both women are emotionally expressive and have the desire to openly share of themselves with a high level of sensitivity and intimacy. When they are together it is hard to imagine that Kelli was not raised by her biological mother. There is warmth and a love that would appear to the uninformed observer, to have been developed over a lifetime of shared experiences.

Even from the beginning, I was always different from my family. I have grown up with them and I love them to death, but I'm so different from them. They have that dry humor that's different from mine. I'm silly. I get that from my biological mother. There are a lot of things that I see in me that are just from being her daughter from birth. I'm so much like her.

Kelli has experienced incredible personal growth in the short time that she has been in contact with her biological mother. She has learned a definition of "mother" that helps her better understand Charlotte as well as how she will "mother" her young daughter.

A mother is someone who nurtures her child. Actually, there are two different kinds of mothers. A mother is somebody who loves you and raises you. There are also mothers who nurture you and help you develop your soul. There are mothers who develop you so that you can be independent.

I have two mothers and most people only have one. I can talk to one mother about one thing and another mother about another thing. I can talk to one about my feelings and she can help me. She lifts me up when I'm down. With my other mother, I can talk about work and career. She's not an emotional person. It's good to have the balance.

Athena and Julia

Power does not mean control over others. That is authority. Power from others must be given to us. We do, however, have individual power that we can decide to give away or to claim for ourselves. Only when we harness and connect to our own inner power are we able to help others find theirs. How we relate to our mother often impacts how we relate to our own daughter. Athena almost gave away her individual power to her mother, Julia. Control, authority and power caused a major rift in their relationship. Becoming a mother has helped Athena to connect to herself, claim her own power and recognize the strength that she has within.

Athena and Julia

When one sees Athena for the first time the immediate and stark impression is that she does not represent any of the traditional and conventional characteristics stereotypical of an Ivy League medical school graduate. Although she is expensive in her taste, she is by no means conservative. Athena is as comfortable in her thigh-length clinging skirt, sexy top, slightly revealing cleavage, and three-inch almost stiletto heels, as she is in her starchy, white, medical jacket. A regular workout program and attention to her diet have resulted in a svelte girlish figure even at the age of forty-something. Her mother, Julia, is an eighty-five-year-old retired social worker. At only five feet tall, Julia has spent a considerable part of her life as an activist: picketing, boycotting, and addressing the wrongdoings of major institutions. Athena is her only daughter. She has two sons and divorced her husband after twenty-nine years of marriage.

"If You Don't Stand For Something, You Will Fall For Anything"

Athena has vivid recollections of her childhood and of Julia during that critical period of her life. She remembers Julia as an individual who was strong in her appreciation of her African and Native American roots. She was a courageous woman who stood up for her beliefs, fought injustices, and rallied around the causes of the disenfranchised. Athena considered Julia as a "pow-

20

erhouse" of a woman who, despite her petite stature, stood tall and dauntless in her attempts to address social and political issues. Julia raised Athena to appreciate her multicultural identity and value her diverse heritage. Though, of a complexion and facial features that would have allowed her to "pass," Julia was clear about her descent and raised Athena to be proud of hers. If there were ever a legitimate reason to confront the establishment in order to protect her definition of her individual rights and the rights of others, Julia was there to take up the cause.

> The school system was very good in telling us about what white people had done. She felt it was very essential that we know about the African and Indian part of us. To this end, she collected books and literature and always made us aware of the achievements of both groups. I attended a Catholic school. I can remember my mother picketing the school board. They had accepted a geography book into the curriculum representing children of the world in a positive fashion, except for the black child. This American child of color was a little boy portrayed with his head buried in a piece of watermelon. She picketed until they removed the book from the curriculum. My mother would picket anybody. She was a very vocal person, a powerhouse.

In many respects Julia was ahead of her time, being somewhat of a feminist in her orientation and views about the role of women in society. For her, women had a right to all of the privileges and opportunities that were available to men. This was certainly not the prevailing female view in her day, but she wasn't worried about being popular. She was worried about being fair. Consequently, Athena, as her only daughter, was raised to have the same aspirations and expectations for her life as Julia set forth for Athena's brothers. Athena felt no sense of gender limitation.

Julia was not only tough in addressing the establishment; she was a devout Catholic and a strict disciplinarian who believed in physical punishment for her children. This tiny woman had no qualms or second thoughts about spanking Athena when she needed to be reprimanded. Even on those occasions, Athena recalls that she was basically fair and most of the time correct in dispensing her wrath.

Overall, Athena had a good childhood that promoted values of strength in her cultural and racial identity, a strong will, outspokenness, and a passion for issues of fairness and equity. Athena learned these qualities well, and gives full credit to Julia for building that foundation.

"YOU CAN'T TEACH AN OLD DOG NEW TRICKS"

Like in her politics, Julia was open-minded and had a liberal attitude in her approach to sex. She had once posed in the nude for an artist, and was uninhibited about her body and her sexuality. As Athena moved to puberty and to womanhood, she was receptive to her emerging sexuality. Athena always felt good about her body and viewed its changes as normal and healthy. Though Julia's behavior around Athena becoming a woman was open, she felt uncomfortable in entertaining conversation on the subject. The primary exception was warning Athena about pregnancy. The scant information that Julia communicated, was approached in a positive and forthcoming manner explaining to Athena that her body would undergo changes and that those changes were natural.

Athena became sexually active in her teens and had several serious intimate relationships while in undergraduate school. Later, while in medical school, Julia allowed Athena and her boyfriend to live together in her home. This was not only her way of acknowledging and accepting Athena's sexuality, but was Julia's method of keeping an eye on her. Later, Athena married, and after divorcing her husband, decided to adopt a daughter, Diana. Having experienced such an open and basically healthy relationship with Julia, Athena never anticipated that becoming a mother would radically change her relationship with her own mother. It was on the issue of childrearing that Athena and Julia parted ways.

> Unfortunately, what happened was that my mother retired. So, she didn't have anything else to do with her time. She wanted to run my life and she wanted to run Diana's life. She had been studying child development. I think that she looked at all the things she would have done differently and wanted to do these things with Diana. But this one was mine. And that eventually made for our separation.

As Julia had aged, she had become narrow minded, somewhat bigoted and much less tolerant than she had been during Athena's youth. She no longer espoused views of multiculturalism and equity. Additionally, encouraged by her child development studies, she had become less of a disciplinarian taking a more permissive and lenient stance on raising children. Athena, living what she had learned from Julia, was attempting to raise Diana within a set of values similar to the more authoritarian principles that had been instilled in her.

This caused a natural clash, which manifested itself negatively in Athena and Julia's relationship. Julia was approaching Diana with her less tolerant and newly learned childrearing theory. Athena, on the other hand, wanted Diana to be a tolerant person, responsible for her own actions and respectful of strong parental discipline. Julia's new behavior caused great conflict for Athena, for Diana, and for the relationship of each to the other.

She persistently and consistently disobeyed my rules. I did not appreciate it and it led to friction with my child. This pulling made my child very nervous and very fractionated. It started when she was really young. I remember every time Diana would go to stay with my mom, when she'd come back, it would take her days just to get back into sync. As time went on, it got worse. But my child is still a child. She's like a bull. She's stubborn. Then when my mother couldn't do much with her, she now wants to hold her to some other standard. She'd been telling her that it was "her way" since she was two years old. I just stopped seeing her, stopped talking to her. My daughter hasn't seen her since she was eight and she's now fifteen.

Athena has struggled with Diana and has been vigilant in her attempt to undo the damage caused by the inconsistency in the messages that Diana has received from Athena and Julia. Resulting from the mixed messages, Diana pressed the envelope many times and experienced serious adjustment problems in her early elementary school days. Athena made a critical decision when these behavior problems began to affect Diana's skill acquisition. Athena believes that what has helped Diana most is that she has spent the past four years in a boarding school. It has been tough for Athena to release her child, but through this experience Diana is learning self-discipline, getting a high-quality education, and experiencing the multicultural world Julia raised Athena to respect and appreciate.

She really has improved. We relate to each other much better these days. I tended to be very controlling and I knew she was reaching a time in her life where she really needed to get out from under me. You get away, you get distance, and then I can get reordered. I pick my battles now. I know I have been a real witch. I have been very strong with her. She needed a strong hand at times. Now we have risen above the physical stuff. I'm glad we've risen above that stage where you have to catch her and spank her and that kind of carrying on. I didn't expect her puberty to disturb me the way it has. It has really rocked my world. My God, just let me get through these next few years with no babies, no pregnancies.

"I Hope You Grow Up And Have Children Just Like You So They Can Drive You Crazy Like You Do Me"

Today Julia is as healthy as one can expect for her eighty-plus years. Her two sons, neither having managed their lives very well, have come home to live with her. Athena doesn't want any part of that scene and has maintained a very distant relationship with Julia. Athena is keenly aware of the changes in personality and values that Julia displayed, as she grew older. As a result, it has made Athena carefully monitor her own behavior particularly related to how she approaches Diana. She works hard to make sure that she maintains a full life with activities and interests that excite her. In this way, she feels she will be less likely to fixate on her child, as Julia attempted to do with Diana.

Having seen her go that way makes me very cautious of keeping my mind open. I keep in touch with where my head is and why it's there. I quiz myself about why I do what I do. As I get older, it has served to provide notice to me so that I'm not trying to correct with Diana's children what I didn't do with her. She wanted to run my life and she wanted to tell me how to run Diana's. It's not going to work. Diana and I went through hell, years of absolute hell, acting out, and horrible stuff. I can say she's much pass that.

When a daughter becomes a mother, the original mother/daughter bond is typically strengthened. Daughters are able to more clearly understand why their mothers did certain things, why some things were so important to them, and what they wanted to accomplish with their actions. Athena expected this outcome when she became a mother. In contrast for Athena and Julia, Athena's move into motherhood caused a rift that the two women have not yet been able to close. At the same time, the rift has been the source of incredible wisdom for Athena as she attempts to provide good mothering for Diana. Athena is using parenting skills, values, and standards that she saw Julia provide and that she viewed beneficial to her own development as a woman. She is also making adjustments to assure that she doesn't make the same mistakes.

What helped me gain a better perspective of my mother and appreciate all of her faults and good points, was becoming a mother. I never would have begun to fathom what she had been through, why she did it, why she was so adamant in certain respects, if I had not had a child. This child is wonderful, and has brought me much closer to an understanding and true appreciation of my mother. But this child is also the reason why we're now not talking.

ANDREA AND LENA

Unconditional love is total acceptance. It is the true "all or nothing" state of relationships. It is not based on meeting expectations that are set by others or on anyone's personal standards or guidelines. We must love ourselves, accept ourselves, and allow ourselves, as well as others, to BE and to BECOME. Only then can we truly experience unconditional love. For Andrea to truly love herself she must first feel free to fully express her true self to her mother Lena. By aligning her actions and feeling and sharing her true self with Lena, Andrea can truly BE and BECOME and experience Lena's unconditional love.

ANDREA AND LENA

Andrea's voice is full of energy and enthusiasm as we begin our early morning conversation. It is over one hundred degrees and she is busy preparing her grill for a cook out she is hosting later in the day at her home in Texas. When asked for her full attention so that we can talk, she requests ten more minutes to complete her task. She then decides to stop and concentrate on our discussion about her life and relationship with her mother, Lena. Andrea is a technical writer with a large international computer company. She is forty-three-years-old, short in stature with a very light complexion and short cropped, curly black hair. She has a warm, engaging smile and a girlish look that is much younger than her chronological age would suggest. Lena, seventy-six years old, is from Jamaica and is a housewife and mother of nine children, two of whom are foster children that she raised from an early age. Andrea is the youngest of the four daughters.

"YOU ARE KNOWN BY THE COMPANY YOU KEEP"

Andrea recalls a warm, loving childhood and family life. She is specific and detailed about aspects of her experiences during this period and describes a cheerful, fun-filled childhood existence. They would frequently go fishing because this was a fun activity that did not cost the large family any money and on the good days, even brought home fresh fish to fry and eat. Andrea still loves to fish. She remembers a childhood with lots of time for playing in a safe, somewhat racially integrated neighborhood. Everyone knew everyone, and neighbors felt responsible for their own, as well as each other's, children. It was a real community that took care of itself.

Even with nine children in the family, Andrea never really wanted for anything. The four sisters were extremely close. They looked out for Andrea and taught her the things that many girls might learn from their mother. Lena was a loving and nurturing person. Although Andrea was well disciplined and received her share of whippings, there was a closeness between Lena and Angela that she finds hard to articulate. Andrea looked up to Lena as a model of strength and kindness. She knew that Lena cared about her and that they loved each other very much. They shared a special bond of affection and attachment, and Andrea was always deeply devoted to Lena.

The love that Lena shared with Andrea was also shared with the other children, their friends, and classmates. Andrea's home was always filled with children. It was the gathering spot for many children in the neighborhood to come, play, and eat. Lena closely watched over her clan and instilled in Andrea a giving, loving, and outgoing spirit. She always told Andrea that she would be known by the company she kept. Lena's concern was that Andrea be surrounded by children that were of similar character and upbringing. She kept a close eye on the company Andrea was keeping.

"There Is No Such Thing As A Little Bit Pregnant"

Unlike her vivid recollections of her childhood, specificity and detail becomes vague and ambiguous when Andrea reaches the stage in her development of becoming a woman. She doesn't recall much at all about those land mines that girls typically encounter and experience as they begin to mature physically and become women.

> *I really don't remember which is interesting. It just doesn't ring a bell for me. I don't know that my mother taught me anything about sex other than I needed to keep my legs closed and my dress down.*

What Andrea does remember is what she considers her first sexual encounter. She was about nine years old when she had a "grinding" experience with a girlfriend. It really wasn't much according to Andrea, just grinding, but she remembers it clearly. When Andrea was fourteen, however, she turned to a male partner and went beyond just grinding. Her second sexual experience and her first heterosexual encounter resulted in pregnancy. She couldn't believe that after the very first time engaging in sexual intercourse, she was pregnant. She was in complete denial over her unlucky and regrettable circumstance. She didn't know what to do, so she did nothing. Eventually, Lena found out about Andrea's condition, and without any discussion or input, sent Andrea to an Aunt in New York. Abortions were legal in New York, but at the time, not in Andrea's home state. Although her father's anger over the pregnancy created a rift that was never to be repaired, Lena focused on fixing Andrea's problem.

Andrea, even at such a young age, knew enough about life to realize that she wasn't prepared to be a mother. Passively, she went along with Lena's decision and aborted her unborn child. Soon after her graduation from high school, but still a teenager, Andrea became pregnant again. This time she made her own decision to abort. She realized that the father of her unborn child was ill equipped to support her. He was also, in Andrea's opinion, not prepared to be part of the storybook family life that Andrea had experienced and envisioned for herself. As Lena had made the decision for Andrea to abort without Andrea's input, Andrea made her decision without input from the man who fathered her unborn child.

"NEVER MISTAKE KINDNESS FOR WEAKNESS"

Andrea credits her mother with teaching the importance of being a nurturing, giving, and loving person in all relationships. Andrea has lived her life accordingly, almost to a fault.

It's interesting because I operate in relationships today in the same manner. I am the one who gives love very freely. Often times it is not reciprocated. My mother would say that people often times mistake kindness for weakness. People try to capitalize on your kindness. I still operate on that method in many situations. Codependency is how I would term it. I'm not sure that I don't seek out people who need to be taken care of to fulfill that need within myself.

At age thirty-one, Andrea learned something else about herself and relationships, which would significantly alter her dream for a "storybook life."

I have a friend that I'm talking with and I have figured out that she is gay. I'm very much attracted to her. I'm trying to figure out how I handle this. How do I deal with it? It's entirely new to me. I don't know what I'm doing. I don't know what I need to be doing. I don't know how to address it. I finally tell her that I am attracted to a woman and I am trying to understand how I deal with it. She said, "Well you should tell her." She said, "You need to address it." So I said, well it's you. You know, for some time we didn't talk about that but it eventually led to a sexual encounter. That was very interesting because it felt so very natural for me. That was really the beginning of it.

Following that encounter Andrea wrote a poem to her lover.

You took me somewhere where wild flowers blossom
Where bees made honey, where the birds sang a sweet melody
I went with you to a place where the sky was always blue
Where butterflies floated, where the sun always shined
Together we rode a hot air balloon that floated on the
 shoulders of the breeze
We sailed high above the ocean, floated far above the trees
And together we swam in a pool of life

"LOVE THE LORD FIRST, LOVE YOURSELF SECOND THEN YOU WILL KNOW WHAT IT IS TO LOVE OTHERS"

More than ten years have passed since Andrea had her first sexual encounter as a lesbian. Today she is still deeply involved with the same woman. This lesbian relationship is by no means the "storybook" relationship she envisioned for herself. There is no husband, wife, two children, German Shepherd, Sports Utility Van, and fenced-in suburban home. During a brief breakup, Andrea experienced one heterosexual encounter, which served to assure her that she was indeed a lesbian. Her partner still questions whether she is truly a lesbian.

There was a point that my friend decided that she didn't think that I was really gay. She did not want me making a change in my life that was going to cause me a lot of heartache and grief. I was told that I was not gay, that I was just experimenting. I found that to be very hurtful. I guess I looked at it as another love rejection. So later, while I was out of town, I met this guy. I thought, okay, let me see if I can make this work. I tried it and it wasn't right. I didn't feel comfortable. So I've been in this relationship for the last ten years.

That was a difficult issue for me to deal with because again, this was my first lesbian encounter. So.how do you process that question? The way I processed it was to try dealing on a heterosexual level, and I felt like I was missing something. The interesting thing that I have found about the lesbian lifestyle is that it's not so much the sex as it is the intimacy. It is being able to share and have somebody understand what you're feeling or why you're feeling it. The emotionalism. There is a lot of communication without words or without touching. It's kind of a bonding.

Five years ago, Andrea and her partner moved away from the state where Andrea's family resides and she became public with her lesbian lifestyle. The relocation was an opportunity to leave the confining environment where everyone knew her and her family. She felt the need to be in a place and in a position with enough anonymity to feel the freedom to be more openly and outwardly gay. She was too inhibited and afraid at home to actively search, explore, and develop an understanding of herself as a lesbian. She needed to move to be true to herself. Today, Andrea is almost totally out. Her brothers, sisters, friends, coworkers and neighbors all know that she is a lesbian. She lives a lesbian lifestyle freely and openly with only one exception...

I've not shared this with my mother. I think at this point and time in her life, what difference does it make? I mean she knows me. I'm her daughter. She loves me. That's not something that she's going to have to deal with me about, so it's not important. She knows my partner and she speaks very highly of her. I just don't think that it's important for her to know. I have decided not to share that with her. I think that if I shared it with her, it would not be an issue. Again, I believe that she loves all of her kids unconditionally. I think, interestingly enough, it may be because of who my mother raised me to be that has allowed me to really be okay with the fact that I am homosexual.

As Andrea grows older and moves more openly and deeply into her life journey as a lesbian, she is continually learning, and she often reflects on her mother's wisdom. She sees a lot of her mother's traits in herself. Like Lena, Andrea is a people lover and enjoys having people around her. She is quite outgoing and is always cooking and entertaining. Her home, like Lena's, is a gathering place for her friends. Like Lena, she is warm, giving, and nurturing in her relationships. Like Lena, she does all types of things for people without them asking and without any obligations attached. She is a very giving person, as Lena taught her to be.

Andrea has never been happier. She attributes this happiness to the freedom she has gained by moving away from her family. She is comfortable with her life as a lesbian. The geographical distance has not diminished her strong sense of family, but has served to give her the space and peace she needed to truly be herself. Though she has not shared her lifestyle with her mother, it was Lena's unconditional love, that gave Andrea the strength to truly acknowledge her sexual preference.

29

I think that moving away from my family was a very empowering thing for me. I now acknowledge that I am a good person. It allowed me to say who Andrea really is. I am very much happy. It was probably the best thing that I could have done. I believe that people are born as they are. Their sexuality is dictated long before they even realize that they think they have sexuality. I think that a lot of people repress those feelings. My mother always said that you couldn't say you dislike something in someone else that you don't see in yourself. That kind of philosophy is one that I have developed since I have come to understand my sexuality. That's something that I learned as a young child. My mother taught me about love, truly, my mother. When I was growing up, we didn't talk about love. There was not a whole lot of "I love you" but love was shared. I felt that my mother was always proud of me no matter what I did or how I did it. I think that my mother looked at all of us as individuals. She knew our shortcomings for sure but it was always very important to me that I was not a disappointment to my mother. I learned that you have to find love within yourself before looking for it externally. A woman must learn to love herself. I don't think that I'm through with that journey but I think that I've come a long way. Be true to yourself. Understand and acknowledge who you are. I think that's regardless of if you are a homosexual or heterosexual.

ELANNA AND SYLVIA

If a man say, I love God, and hateth his brother, he is a liar: for he
that loveth not his brother whom he hath seen, how can he love God
whom he hath not seen? (1 John 4:20) Elanna hated the life that Sylvia
lived and the man she shared that life with. She pledged to herself that
Sylvia's fate would never be hers. From Sylvia, Elanna learned how to
put aside her hate and anger and to fully appreciate the gift of life and
love.

ELANNA AND SYLVIA

Elanna had described herself as being "full-figured." Sharing that trait, it
was no surprise in the crowded entrance to the church following the early
morning service that our eyes met in instant recognition. Elanna was somewhat tense on that hot summer morning as we drove the brief distance to a
nearby restaurant. Elanna, Sylvia's youngest daughter, is the proud mother of
two daughters and a son. As we were seated in the restaurant rapidly over-
flowing with others from our church service, the thought occurred that it was
a mistake to meet in such a public place. How would we conduct an interview
concerning such private matters with all the people and all the noise? Later,
it would seem as though we were the only two people in the entire restaurant.
As we engaged in light discussion while awaiting our order, this beautiful thir-
ty-eight-year-old, chocolate brown woman began to relax. Her warm smile
told me that she was okay. She was wearing an African outfit in my favorite
color purple. Elanna works in a home for behaviorally-disordered young people. She grew up in a large city in the Midwest with her mother and father and
six other children. Her mother, Sylvia, has been dead for thirteen years and
was originally from Tennessee.

*She was very sweet and would do anything for her kids, anything at all. She did
not work outside the home. My father did not allow her to work. He was a macho
man, a Neanderthal type, when it came to women. She would walk down the street
and hold her head down. I remember this very, very sweet, and humble woman. She
was a very beautiful woman.*

"IT TAKES A FRIEND AND AN ENEMY TO REALLY HURT YOU. THE ENEMY TO SAY SOMETHING REALLY ROTTEN ABOUT YOU AND THE FRIEND TO TELL YOU ABOUT IT."

Elanna spent her childhood in an environment of abject poverty and economic despair. Her memories are of living in tenement apartments without heat, water, electricity, or sometimes food. She grew up being mocked, taunted, ridiculed and even beaten by other children who were insensitive to the fact that Elanna did not have decent clothing or could not afford to buy or even bring her lunch to school. She was talked about and humiliated.

Sylvia did the very best that she could to raise her family properly notwithstanding the poverty that surrounded them. Elanna was brought up in the Catholic church, and Sylvia made sure that all of her children attended church regularly. She was not as concerned about the denomination, location, or the congregation; as she was about wanting her children in church on Sunday mornings. Elanna attended Catholic schools as well, and since the family was very poor, the children were not tuition paying students. Their level of poverty was such that they were identified in the community as a family that required special assistance and support. The local Catholic school essentially took them on as a project. The school provided not only free education, but free lunches and many times clothing and other essentials that were required. In return, Elanna and her siblings had the responsibility to perform various tasks such as cleaning up the lunchroom and classrooms after school and during recess. These tasks further isolated Elanna from her peers and it made her even more acutely aware of her poverty and how different her life seemed to be from that of the other students. In spite of all of this, Elanna grew up believing that a good education was the key to removing herself from poverty.

It was terrible. It was really awful going to school every day. It was really kind of bad because we were so very poor. Other kids would come to school dressed nice and everything; we didn't have that. We would come with no lunch. In the winter time it gets dark around four o'clock, so if you didn't get your homework done as soon as you got home from school, you weren't getting it done because you couldn't see. There were no lights. Some of the nuns would feel sorry for us and give us hot lunches and that's what we would eat a lot. The priest and nun at school felt sorry for me so they took me under their wings. They said I had the potential to be something.

Not only did Elanna endure poverty as a child; she endured the pain of observing Sylvia's regular beatings at the hands of her husband. These beatings provide perhaps the most vivid recollections from Elanna's childhood.

Sylvia was married to a man who abused her almost daily. He would beat her if there was no hot food at dinnertime, knowing that there was no gas for cooking or possibly no food. He would beat Sylvia if he thought another man looked at her too closely, even though her beauty naturally caught the attention of men. He would beat her if he was drunk, which was often, and he'd beat her if he was sober. Elanna talks about those beatings with tears in her eyes and recalls how she would cry and be so very afraid. Sylvia rarely called the police because she was also afraid. She couldn't leave her husband because she had no place to go. Her family lived in Tennessee, and she knew that any arrest would be brief and would only cause another beating when her husband was released. Sylvia humbly endured, and Elanna helplessly observed.

He brought her up here and he could do what he wanted to her. Several times he would put all of us out of the house. It didn't matter if we were dressed or if we had shoes on. It really didn't matter to him. Other times, he would put her out and she would have to sneak back. She'd have to hide under the bed and she would stay there all night. I know that was the reason she always walked down the street with her head low. She was embarrassed. This was the kind of stuff he did to her. This is how he treated her, and the type of life she lived.

"IF YOU WANT TO KEEP SOMETHING A SECRET, DO IT ALONE"

Elanna did not have any conversations with Sylvia about her sexuality or development as she reached puberty. Sylvia was shy and this subject was taboo in her household. So Elanna became a woman while still a little girl. Her father introduced her to sex, molesting her at the age of ten and forcing her to caress his penis. Elanna remembers that occasion well. It was her first introduction to the male anatomy and to the potential for yet a different kind of abuse. She remembers another incident at the age of twelve. Elanna was beginning to physically show signs of her womanness and her breasts were just developing. While at home alone with her father, he sucked her breasts to the point of badly bruising them. Elanna knew instinctively that something was wrong. She was frightened, too frightened to tell her mother because she did not want to see her beaten or be beaten herself. Her father told her not to tell anyone, and Elanna felt the need to keep his secret.

That really scared me, upset me. I didn't know how to tell her. I knew something was wrong. He told me not to tell her. I was scared. I didn't know what would happen. I didn't want her to get a beating because of something I did. She kept asking and I told her that I was raking in the yard and the end of the rake hit me in the chest. She didn't believe me. She went checking down the line of all of my brothers. Then she said, "Did he do it?" I guess I looked at her stupid. She just grabbed me and held me. She said, "Don't worry about it ever again." I don't think she ever brought that to him because she was afraid. She did the only thing she could do; she never left my sister or me alone with him again. I think that's why my mother kept me under her wing so much.

Since Sylvia did not discuss matters regarding Elanna's development as a woman, Elanna learned about her sexuality the way she could, in the streets, from girl friends and later through personal trial and error. She waited longer than most of her peers to explore her sexuality. She had a real fear that she would become pregnant. Although Sylvia had been able to provide the blockage necessary to keep her husband from further sexual abuse of Elanna, she was not able to keep him from his verbal abuse. In his anger and drunkenness he would accuse Elanna of sexual promiscuity, call her a whore, and in other ways position Elanna as sexually active well before she began her self-described "trial and error" sex education. Elanna delayed her experimentation with sex at least in part because she never wanted to do anything that would strengthen her father's position. She did not want him to be proven right. She certainly didn't want him to have cause to think she was available for him. When Elanna did venture into a sexual relationship, she chose the cutest boy at college, a basketball player who was also known as a ladies man. Elanna didn't care that Mr. Campus had a reputation for sleeping around, because she had set a goal to not leave college as a virgin. She and Sylvia never did have a conversation about this critical aspect of her development as a woman.

"DO AS I SAY, NOT AS I DO"

As Elanna got older, and married, Sylvia would always tell her not to use her as a model to emulate. Later, Elanna understood what this continual caution meant. She came to understand that Sylvia was telling her not to ever be helpless or placed in situations where she would be subjected to any type of abuse. She'd always tell her, "don't be like me." Elanna vowed to herself never to marry an abusive man. Her sixteen-year marriage is quite different from Sylvia's. Her mother's wisdom and life led Elanna to secure herself by making sure that she was properly educated and prepared to take care of herself and her children.

I'm always employed because regardless of how nice he is, it's like in the back of my mind I fear.

Fear for Elanna, fear for Sylvia. Elanna, now a young woman with her own family wonders why her mother didn't leave her abusive husband and situation. One reason may be that during this period of time there were few shelters for abused women or other places to seek refuge. But later, either of her daughters would have gladly taken her in. When her children became young adults, Sylvia, decided that she wanted to return to school and ultimately open a day care center. She was doing well, making grades, and the more it seemed she might be successful, the more the abuse, the more beatings, the more jealousy from her husband.

After a particularly brutal beating, Sylvia left home for about a month and lived with Elanna's sister. But she returned home, telling her daughters that her husband had promised to change. She wanted to give him that opportunity. That very same weekend, Elanna, attempting to reach Sylvia, who did not have a telephone, called a cousin's house that lived near Sylvia. Sylvia was there on a cold, snowy night, barefoot, and beaten. Elanna immediately went to her mother and called the police. Furious, and crying and as the police took her father away, Elanna shouted to Sylvia, "I hate him, I hate him." She promised Sylvia that the next time he beat her she was going to shoot him and kill him. Hearing this, Sylvia, in her own pain from her beating, slapped Elanna so hard that Elanna literally saw stars. The message Elanna received from Sylvia that night is crystal clear to her more than thirteen years later.

She said she didn't ever want to hear me say that. She said, "You hate what he does. Love him because he's your father." That has always stuck with me. I just shut up then and helped her pack her stuff, but that is something that has always stuck in my mind.

After that beating, Elanna recalls that her father was in jail less than thirty days, and as usual, Sylvia returned home to him. The next time Sylvia was beaten, there was no more leaving and coming back. Hardly clothed and likely raped, she died from injuries to her head inflicted with a two by four. He beat her until he killed her. Her neighbors heard her screams and her pleas for him to stop. Sylvia was pronounced dead upon arrival of the police and paramedics. Since there was no heat in the house, her body was too cold for the authorities to know how long she had actually been dead before her body was found.

When I went to see her at the hospital, they didn't want me to see her. I just went off. I told them that I was going to check every room until I found her. They pulled the cover down to let me see her. She had marks around her neck and around her wrists, two big gashes in her forehead and a look on her face like she was asking for help. She was scared to death. There was a look of fear on her face. It took everything out of me. I just left for a few days. I left my husband and my children. I was at a lost, alone, not knowing what to do at that point. I think I was too close to her. Sometimes I think that God took her from me. Maybe he was jealous because the way I should feel about God, I was feeling about her. I know God is not a jealous God. Sometimes I think about how life is now. It's like, if she were here, I wouldn't be as productive as I am now. I do honestly believe that God did take her for the betterment of my life. So I could do what he had planned for me. He had lots of things planned for me. If she were in my life I would not have done them.

If she didn't live that type of life, I would have no lesson to live from or anything to give to anybody else. I work with children very well. I have no problems with that and I love it. I think it's because of all the adversity she had in her life.

"Two Wrongs Don't Make A Right"

For thirteen years Elanna did not deal with Sylvia's death. She continued to run away from it, to somehow put it aside and try to forget all that she had seen, heard, and felt in her abusive surroundings. Recently she was moved to address her mother's death and saw an opportunity to honor Sylvia. She decided that this was the time to put closure around Sylvia's horrible life and untimely death.

This is the first Mother's Day that I went out. I actually got a Mother's Day outfit. I wanted an all white outfit. This is going to be a tribute to my mother, this Mother's Day. I don't care what nobody else is wearing. I'm wearing my own white outfit and sitting right up front where I always sit. This is a Mother's Day tribute to my mom, I told my children, I really feel bad that all these years since she's been passed. It was always a depressing time for me. It's not depressing anymore. I told them that.

Elanna has a message for her own children and for other women and children who might face the poverty, despair and violence of her childhood. That message, that wisdom that comes from Sylvia is about loving one another.

I am not hating him. I hate what he did. I'd be stupid to say I didn't hate what he did to her. You have to learn how to cross that fence. You hate what he does and you can feel love for him as a person because he is my father.

Hate is such a strong word. How are you going to hate something and expect to love everything that God gives you? How can you love God and say that you hate somebody else? You don't know that person; you just know their behavior.

There are a lot of people that live similar lives, involved with husbands, and nobody ever says anything. Years later you sit down and talk it over with a girlfriend or some-one. You find that their life was much like yours. All this time you thought everything was great. So many people out there are just like we were. It gives me chills. It does-n't get talked about. There is some young girl who is going through the very same thing I went through and she thinks that she's the only one. She doesn't have any-body to talk to.

Elanna wrote a poem to help close the door on her past, cleanse the hate for her father, and most importantly, acknowledge and express appreciation to Sylvia for her love, her strength, and her wisdom.

This Is For All The Times Mama (Sylvia)

This is for all the times when the food had to bypass
your mouth and come straight into mine
Thanks Mama and Happy Mother's Day

This is for the nights that were so cold and wrong
I found you crying all alone and you wiped your tears away
Ever so fast you refused to let me see that pain last
You grabbed me tight in your arms and apologized
for all my hurts and harm
Thanks Mama and Happy Mother's Day

This is for the nights you spent under the beds
being repeatedly beat with his fist in your head.
You told me don't hate him, hate what he does
Hate is too strong
Baby you've got to love
Thanks Mama and Happy Mother's Day

This is for taking that last beat down with no one
around to save you
And I know you don't want me to hate him,
do you? You taught me to love
Thanks Mama and Happy Mother's Day

This is for the good times that I know we had
I am so sorry but it is hard to be glad
For on this day my heart is very sad
Please forgive me my Dear Mother
many tears drop from my eyes
As I rise from my knees and
look towards the sky

I thank God with a fresh twinkle in my eye
Oh my Sweet Mama when my turn comes
Our souls will meet again
OUR SOULS WILL MEET AGAIN

Excuse me Mama, I think I just stopped crying
My heart is no longer dying
Now I will continue to pray
Because that is something you taught me to do each and everyday

THANKS MAMA. I LOVE YOU. HAPPY MOTHER'S DAY

GERALDINE AND MAGGIE

Choice is a powerful tool for life. Each of us has the choice to create our own reality. We are neither forced to live by the circumstances of our past, nor hindered by the perceived limitations of our future. Geraldine did not make choices in her life soon enough to assure that her mother Maggie's choices would not set the pattern for her life. Geraldine now realizes that she can and must determine her own destiny. She knows that she must make different choices and learn from generations of mistakes.

GERALDINE AND MAGGIE

Geraldine is going grocery shopping after our early Saturday morning meeting. Looking youthful and comfortable in her denim shorts, she is a stately, six-foot tall woman. She has deep dark brown skin and short hair as white as freshly fallen snow. Geraldine has recently celebrated her fiftieth birthday and is proud of the fact that she is not only a mother, but a grandmother as well. Geraldine is a divorcé and works as a consultant for an employment placement firm. Geraldine is from Georgia and has two children: one daughter and one son. Maggie, her mother, is eighty-years-old and is a retired domestic worker who lives in a nursing home. Maggie was the oldest daughter in a family of eight children. Maggie's father had nine other children in an extramarital relationship. All of these children lived in the same small town, and as such, Maggie grew up in an extended family of seventeen children. Maggie married late in life. She was thirty years old when her first child, Geraldine, was born. Maggie really never had a childhood. When Maggie was thirteen years old, her mother died. As the oldest daughter, Maggie had to assume responsibility for the care of her seven siblings. A physically beautiful woman, Maggie was also very shy and withdrawn. She never socialized or dated because her life was filled with the awesome responsibility of being a surrogate mother and working as a domestic to make ends meet.

"YOU ARE WHO YOU SLEEP WITH"

Geraldine has graphic memories of life growing up in a small southern town. When she describes Maggie, she focuses on her bashful and reserved personality. Geraldine says that Maggie *"didn't talk at all."* Maggie was a woman of very few words, quite introverted and socially withdrawn. Geraldine, on the other hand, was an extrovert, much like her philandering father. In addition to their personality differences, Geraldine and Maggie were also quite different in their physical appearances. Geraldine was tall, and very dark skinned. She also had kinky hair, and her distinctly African-American features closely matched those of her father. Maggie, in contrast, was of average height, and fair in complexion. She had what would have been called "good hair," and sharp facial features. Geraldine believes that the physical and personality differences between her and Maggie created an early breach in their relationship. Maggie was strict and wanted to keep Geraldine very close to home. Geraldine just wanted to be free. Mother and daughter were always in conflict and they constantly engaged in both physical and verbal confrontations.

The fights between Geraldine and Maggie were not the only fights in the household. Geraldine's father was a drinker and an abuser. While Maggie quietly cared for her children, worked, and spent any spare time in church, Geraldine's father was rarely home, especially on the weekends. It was no secret to either Geraldine or Maggie, that he had intimate relationships with other women. Geraldine once thought that it was normal for a man to leave his home and family on Friday and not return until late on Sunday evening. Geraldine felt that she was growing up in a typical household. After all, they owned a house; they had a car and her father worked. This was all she knew and this was how she thought a family and a marriage functioned. Geraldine recognized, however, that the severe beatings Maggie endured were not normal. When she was seven years old, Geraldine's world and Maggie's life would change dramatically.

What I remember in those last years leading up to that time, was my mother running through the streets in the middle of the night. We would have on pajamas. She'd grab us out of bed and we'd run down the streets to a neighbor's home. I guess she was just fed up or afraid. It got to be really brutal. My mother's face looked horrible come Monday mornings. One night after one of those real brutal fights, she took us to a neighbor's house. My father had lain down to sleep. It was the weekend and he was drunk. After my mother took us from the house, she went to her best girlfriend and borrowed a shotgun. She came back. He was on the couch asleep. She unloaded the gun on him. She killed him. My mother was sent away for five years.

"WE ARE THE MASTERS OF WHAT WE KEEP TO OURSELVES, THE SLAVES OF WHAT WE SAY"

The death of her father traumatized and frightened the seven-year-old. Geraldine remembers the battered, toothless face of her beautiful mother covering the front page of the local newspaper. She remembers the strange looks and the cruel remarks made by those around her. Initially, Maggie's sisters took custody of Geraldine and her brother and tried very hard to protect them from the stigma associated with the murder. Of course, in such a small southern community, everyone knew about this woman who had, in cold blood, unloaded every bullet in her shotgun into the body of her sleeping husband.

School was horrible for Geraldine. Children taunted her and called her mother a murderer and a jailbird. Geraldine did not attend her father's funeral nor was she informed on the events of Maggie's criminal trial. After Maggie was found guilty, the state awarded Geraldine to her father's family and during her mother's incarceration she lived with her paternal grandmother. One might expect that this would be a poor environment for Geraldine, being placed in the home of the mother of the deceased. Quite to the contrary, Geraldine's paternal grandmother loved her very much and treated her with love and kindness. Geraldine assumes that her grandmother must have known that her son was abusive toward Maggie. Her grandmother was so loving and understanding that she even welcomed Maggie to her home for a brief time when she was released from prison.

When she returned from prison, Maggie was faced with the challenge of raising her children in a hostile community. The stigma in the school and community had not ended so Maggie moved her family to another Southern city. Geraldine, with her father's personality and looks, was a constant reminder to Maggie of his abuse and of the murder.

I reminded my mother of my father because I was dark, an extrovert and I talked all the time. She would tell me to shut up, call me a monkey, and say that I was ugly. Every day of my life when I was growing up, my mother called me ugly. This was after she had killed my father and gone to prison and come back. What I realize is that she took out her hurt and anger on me. I always felt that I was so ugly. I slumped because I was so tall. Even in my prom picture, I was slumped over. We fought every single day. It was a constant thing that you're ugly and you act ugly. You act just like you look and you're a horrible person. This is what she told me constantly.

Going to prison did not change Maggie's introverted characteristics. She remained the silent, withdrawn personality that she always was. The murder was never discussed.

Until this day my mother has never talked about the murder or her prison time. As I grew older, I realized what pain she must have been in. Not only physical, emotional and mental pain, but also the embarrassment of walking around with your face bruised and battered. My mother was so private and she was so beautiful. But she kept all of that in. Until this day, she's kept all that stuff in. She never went to see a psychiatrist or anything. It's never mentioned. It's like an unspoken thing. Nobody, nobody talks about the fact that my mother killed my father.

Since Maggie was quiet and withdrawn, she did not talk much to Geraldine about her physical maturation as a woman. Maggie was so private, that Geraldine never even saw her undressed. Once, she accidentally walked into Maggie's bedroom while she was getting dressed. Maggie had on a full slip and her other undergarments. Maggie was startled and embarrassed and quickly covered her body and hid herself from the view of her only daughter. Maggie told Geraldine nothing about the start of her menstrual and even after it's onset, she had little to say. It is not clear to Geraldine whether they were too poor to purchase sanitary napkins or perhaps they were unavailable, but Maggie's response to the onset of Geraldine's menstrual was to simply show her how to fold and pin the old rags that were used as sanitary napkins. Maggie never explained why Geraldine was having this experience and told her only that it would happen monthly and that she should stay away from boys. This was the extent of Geraldine's sex education.

With this background of limited knowledge and low self-esteem, it is not surprising that Geraldine, at eighteen years old and still in high school, found herself pregnant following her first sexual encounter. Maggie tried to abort the pregnancy by making Geraldine drink some type of homemade concoction. The remedy didn't lead to an abortion. It led to the birth of a very sickly, premature son. A year later, Geraldine moved north with her infant son.

"MARRY IN HASTE, REGRET IN LEISURE"

The epitome of the stereotypical southern bred country girl, Geraldine now found herself in the big northern city. She quickly met a man, and decided to marry. Although she knew that her husband had abused his former wife, he had convinced Geraldine that she was different and that their relationship was different. Geraldine was certain that whatever happened with the former wife was due to circumstances the ex-wife had created. She believed that the ex-wife most likely deserved her beatings. In a way, Geraldine married her father.

Whatever troubled her husband in his work or in the streets would be transferred to Geraldine and she would be beaten. One positive thing that he did however, was adopt her infant son and later together they had a daughter, Taniesha. Geraldine found herself living Maggie's life with two children and an abusive husband.

Like Maggie's family, Geraldine's family was perceived as the perfect little suburban family; a boy, a girl, a house, a car and a job. She had a wonderful family image on the outside. Inside as in Maggie's case, resided another beaten and abused mother and a daughter to observe the same horror that Geraldine had seen with Maggie. The cycle continued. Taniesha was a very difficult child and resisted all the efforts that Geraldine put forth on her behalf. There were periods when Taniesha became so abusive toward Geraldine, that she actually was fearful of her. Taniesha experienced drugs, numerous abortions, shoplifting, jail time and the birth of two children without benefit of a marriage.

Taniesha said that I verbally abused her and made her feel bad. I think that as a mother you don't realize it. You're angry and you don't see it. Now I can see some of my mother's frustrations and anger. I didn't think I took my anger out with my daughter. I went to counseling for two years to get my self-esteem balanced and checked. I didn't think I abused Taniesha. But maybe my verbal behavior was a form of abuse. I took such good care of my kids. It should not have had that type of effect on Taniesha, but it did. Taniesha says that she's just angry at the world. She doesn't know what she's angry about. It wasn't like she was deprived or anything.

Geraldine eventually divorced her husband. She looked carefully at the life she was leading and saw Maggie's life being recreated. She was afraid that if the pattern of abuse continued, she might take the same path as Maggie and kill her husband. When these thoughts started to occur, Geraldine knew it was time to leave. She has been single now for more than fifteen years and regrets that she didn't leave her husband sooner. She also sees clearly the negative impact that her marriage had on Taniesha.

If I could go all the way back I would not have married that man, that's the first thing. My mother knew it was happening, but said to me you can't come here. She said that men like him come and kill everybody in the house and that someone has to stay alive to take care of the children. That's what my mother told me. When I finally decided to get my divorce, it was after a horrible weekend. I did not love him anymore, and I was no longer afraid of him. You see, I was afraid of him and he knew

43

that. Abusers work off of fear. They know that you are afraid of them. I was no longer afraid of him and I knew that if I didn't leave I was going to kill him. I didn't want to put my children through what my brother and I went through, the stigma of that. I did not want my kids to have to go through that. So I left.

"YOU KNOW WHAT'S BACK THERE, BUT YOU DON'T KNOW WHAT'S OUT THERE. LOOK AHEAD, DON'T LOOK BACK"

Geraldine has never had a healthy relationship with a man, although she now knows through observing others that such relationships can exist. She has worked hard on improving low self-esteem, but still struggles with that part of her identity. What she has created in lieu of good male/female or romantic relationships is solid friendships. She also spends an enormous amount of time focused on her granddaughters. These relationships provide tremendous gratification.

Growing older has been good for Geraldine. As her self-esteem continues to grow, and with the help of counseling, she looks better and feels better about herself. She is successful in her work and receives personal and financial rewards for her extra efforts. For the past seven years, she has had primary responsibility for Maggie's care. Maggie, now suffering from dementia, is in a nursing home that's primarily paid for by Geraldine. Geraldine visits regularly and frequently brings Maggie to her home for weekends and holidays. As Geraldine ages, she finds that she is becoming more like Maggie, staying home a lot and toning down that extroverted aspect of her personality that Maggie so despised. She acknowledges that she has learned and gained from Maggie in spite of the turmoil they experienced as mother and daughter. She loves Maggie but feels deep sorrow and sympathy for her and the difficult life she has led.

Geraldine's relationship with Taniesha is still quite rocky but somewhat better than it was during her teenage years. Geraldine worries that Taniesha's daughters are not growing up in a safe, healthy, nurturing, and loving environment. She also worries about her own future, and wonders who will care for her as she ages and becomes less equipped to care for herself. She is not confident that Taniesha will be prepared to accept such a challenge. Geraldine wants to continue to learn and to grow, and to pass on her wisdom to Taniesha and to her granddaughters.

I don't want Taniesha to take care of me. Taniesha is unstable. I can't see it being Taniesha. But maybe, since everybody comes full circle, it might be Taniesha. I love my mother dearly. I feel so bad that my mother did not have a good life. Now, I want to make sure that she has a decent life. When I grew up I guess I loved my mother but we just didn't like each other. The same thing is true with Taniesha and I. We've realized that we are different. I think that's part of the mother and daughter relationship.

We are our mothers; we do exactly the same things. The key to it is mothers being able to accept their daughters as people, as who they are. We constantly try to make our daughters into what we want them to be. In fact, sometimes we try to live vicariously through our daughters. Since I didn't go to college, I wanted my daughter to go to college. Since I didn't marry the right person, I wanted my daughter to marry the right person. I think that's what makes us crazy. That is what pushes our daughters away. We are so adamant about it. Because we are mothers we want the best for them. Because we love them. Because we love them so much.

IVANNA AND LOIS

Speaking about and doing are very different actions. However, the more we speak about something, the closer we can come to doing it. If we speak more about loving, nurturing and caring, we can come closer to behaving that way. Even with love there is no guarantee of a happy childhood or a fulfilling life. Actions and behaviors buttressed the love that Ivanna felt from her mother, Lois. Ivanna learned that the blessings of life are multiplied when your mother loves you, is your friend and always *has your back*.

IVANNA AND LOIS

The view is breathtaking from this lakeshore condominium on the blistering Sunday afternoon of the meeting with Ivanna and Lois.   Ivanna is petite, and her tiny form and youthful short-coifed Afro hairstyle belie the fact that she is the fifty-four-year-old mother of two adult sons. She is a business owner and a college professor. She is the second child and only daughter born to Lois. Lois, originally from Alabama, fits perfectly in this beautiful environment because at eighty-one years young, she is still so beautiful. This tiny, spry, white-haired woman dressed in a fashionable denim dress authoritatively places herself at the head of the large dining room table where she, undoubtedly, feels most comfortable. With her tiny arms crossed tightly around her chest and a penetrating stern expression in her eyes, she cautiously observes her guest with an air of suspicion. Her eyes are not at all subtle and clearly reveal that she is questioning the purpose and intent of this conversation. Iva appears somewhat perplexed at her mother's almost defensive positioning. However, she is always the respectful daughter and she is obviously not going to challenge this pint-sized tower of strength.

"DON'T LET WHAT OTHERS EAT MAKE YOU SICK"

Lois was not always the picture of health that she presents today. As a young woman, she was confronted with tuberculosis, isolated, and confined to a sanitarium for thirteen months.   Additionally, she experienced the removal of three quarters of her lungs and seven ribs. The fact that she was able to give birth to Ivanna defied the pessimistic predictions of Lois' doctors who had assured her that she would never be able to have children. Lois was twenty-seven years old when Ivanna was born. This was quite late for women in the mid-1940s. Ivanna was a difficult delivery. Throughout her life, she was reminded of this fact. Lois always jokingly told her, "Your brother was like a bowel movement and you came feet first and you've been giving me hell ever since." Ivanna's entrance into the world was so difficult that Lois was actually pronounced dead on the operating table.

Ivanna and Lois share similar stories about their childhoods and of their respective relationships with their mothers. They are both acutely aware of how their lives truly demonstrate the strength of the mother/daughter bond and how wisdom is transmitted intergenerationally.

Lois recalls a very loving early life as the only child of a wise and sacrificing mother, and she continued this pattern as she raised Ivanna.

> The blessing that I know I have, that she is responsible for and that is amazing to me how rare it occurs is that I had a happy childhood. I had an absolutely happy childhood. I can now stand up in church and testify about being happy as a child. As long as I did what they expected me to do. I was a free spirit. I felt like I really had a childhood. That's a real blessing.

Ivanna was raised by a mother and influenced by a grandmother who took great pride in their heritage as strong, beautiful African-American women. Lois took great pride in her appearance and in maintaining her personal dignity as a woman and as an African-American. She believed that her role as a mother was critical, and she was self-sacrificing, in raising Ivanna. Even though the family may have been considered poor from an economic perspective, Ivanna never thought of herself that way. Lois always provided for her needs. She knows also that her upbringing was rich in terms of love, nurturing, and spiritual guidance.

"DON'T BE AN EDUCATED FOOL, ALL BOOK SENSE AND NO COMMON SENSE"

Lois was always there when Ivanna needed her, whether intervening on Ivanna's behalf to fight against racist practices in the schools or providing advice and guidance to make sound decisions. She taught Ivanna to truly value education.

Although Lois' mother only completed eighth grade and in spite of the attitude of Lois' father that education was wasted on girls, Lois was encouraged to continue her education and she completed high school. She impressed upon Ivanna the importance of educating herself as fully as possible, of valuing learning, and of having the confidence that she could accomplish anything that she committed herself to. Lois not only talked about the importance of education, she involved herself actively by working in the Parent Teachers Association and other education-related organizations. Ivanna, strongly internalizing this value, was a very advanced student who studied hard and excelled in her educational pursuits. For Ivanna, getting a good education and attending college was non-negotiable. Ivanna remembers that against her wishes, Lois insisted that she take typing. Being the scholarly type, Ivanna retorted that typing was for secretaries and she had no plans to be anyone's secretary. Of course, Lois won this battle and ironically, it was Ivanna's typing skills that helped her earn money to pay her college tuition. Ivanna has never stopped educating herself.

Though education was critical, both Ivanna and Lois were raised with the wisdom that it was not enough; one must also learn common sense. Lois taught Ivanna that some people get Ph.D. degrees but forget to get the C.S. or common sense degree. She would jokingly tell Ivanna that a B.S. can stand for bull stuff, an M.S. for mule stuff and a Ph.D. for piled high and deep. Ivanna's interpretation of this humorous portrayal of advanced education was not only that education was critical for African-Americans, but that it was worthless if not grounded in the realities of life. Further, Ivanna learned from Lois that it was insufficient to simply acquire education and knowledge for your personal development, it was equally important that it be shared with the community. Ivanna has earned her Ph.D., and uses her talents in a variety of ways to serve the broader African-American community. This "give back" attitude in general, is also intergenerational as Ivanna and Lois were both raised by mothers who were active in causes that enhanced the African-American community.

"SEEING IS DIFFERENT FROM BEING TOLD, PRACTICE WHAT YOU PREACH"

Ivanna successfully completed high school and continued to use Lois as her primary role model for womanhood. Even though quite outspoken on most matters, Lois was reserved and modest as she approached Ivanna about matters related to her development as a woman. Considering the topic of sex to be somewhat dirty and taboo, Lois directed Ivanna to books and instructed her to go to the library to find specific readings related to this subject. On other matters, it was not books, but the strong and positive example that Ivanna observed. Ivanna learned about strength and the phenomenal ability and capacity that African-American women have to resist defeat. She learned about sacrificial behavior and being non-negotiable on matters related to the importance of protecting your self-esteem and human dignity. There were always examples for Ivanna to emulate.

One incident that comes to mind is on occasion when my grandmother, a domestic, couldn't work. She sent my mother to work for her that evening to serve the dinner. My mother walked over to the house to do the cooking, as my grandmother had instructed her. After getting the dinner ready the woman rang the bell for my mother to serve. Well that was just it. My mother was not going to respond to no bell ringing. So she left the woman sitting up in her dining room waiting for her guests to be served. My momma was on her way back home.

Lois also taught Ivanna, by her example, the importance of faith, nurturing, and love. These lessons were very important to Ivanna, as she became a woman and fell in love while still in college. Although Lois objected, Ivanna wanted to marry after completing her first year in college, and marry is exactly what she did. Ivanna's husband had already graduated from college, and even though Lois liked him, she thought him too old for her daughter. She wanted desperately to see Ivanna complete college and felt this would be less likely if she married and started a family. Lois insisted that the new bride and groom promise her that Ivanna would complete her college education. Ivanna kept her promise and she also bore a son. When he was less than one year-old, Ivanna's husband died in a tragic drowning accident. It was during this period that the faith, nurturing, and love of Lois became most critical in Ivanna's life.

It was very natural for me to dig very deeply into her example of strength and faith. On an emotional level, and as a mother, she also felt the necessity to bring me back into the incubator. This was an opportunity to reclaim me as a child. I had to adjust to what that meant. I was somewhere between the fact that I am not a child, that I can never come back home as a child, but I am dependent and in need of your nurturing and love.

"A FOOL AND HIS MONEY SOON PART WAYS"

Lois sent the message to Ivanna to be independent as a woman and in her relationships with men. This started early as Lois made sure that Ivanna had her own bus fare whenever she went on dates, and later, when she attempted to instill in Ivanna the need to keep separate money from her spouse. Lois had learned this lesson from her mother, so it was natural that she would want to share this wisdom with Ivanna. When Lois' mother died, the family found a separate checking account that her husband knew nothing about and Lois too, kept her private "stash."

One of the most significant arguments we've had, and there's probably only been about five in our relationship, had to do with me the weekend before my wedding. She said, "Well, I've got one more thing to discuss with you and that is the need for you to have a separate checking account that your husband doesn't know about." I went off. I said, I don't understand why you are saying this to me. Don't you trust him? She said it had nothing to do with trust, it was about common sense. You have to protect yourself. I told her I'm not going to marry no man I can't trust. That was her attempt to forewarn me about men.

"I BROUGHT YOU INTO THIS WORLD AND I CAN TAKE YOU OUT"

Although in their mid-fifties and early eighties respectively, neither Ivanna nor Lois think much about aging. Recently, Lois had triple by-pass surgery and a near heart attack. She is living with Ivanna as she moves toward complete recovery. Again, and as always, she demonstrated for Ivanna her capacity to defy the odds, risk defeat and her tremendous strength. Ivanna observed this poignantly when Lois was able to leave the hospital ahead of a fifty-year-old man who had entered the hospital at the same time and with the same condition.

Lois thinks that a part of her lack of focus on aging is because she surrounds herself with younger people, including Ivanna and her friends. Since Lois hasn't really focused on aging, she hasn't shared any particular wisdom with Ivanna about how life changes as a woman ages. Lois always taught Ivanna as her mother had taught her, of the importance of women protecting their self-dignity and their reputation. She also passed on to Ivanna an abundance of simple wit and wisdom. Many times Lois would remind Ivanna that she brought her into this world and that she could take her out. Lois still feels that she has the right to challenge Ivanna and she does occasionally playfully exercise it. She knows that the "I brought you into the world" reminder is one Ivanna no longer needs. Ivanna has treated her mother with the respect and dignity she has deserved for bringing her into this world and preparing her for her life journey. Lois has provided Ivanna with an uncompromising sense of self-esteem and self-worth, and an attitude that she could and should strive to have anything and be everything she desired in life, both materially and spiritually. Lois has consistently delivered the message, in both her words and her deeds, that the world belongs to Ivanna.

She allowed me to know that "she had my back". I think it's a great blessing to have a mother who is a friend. That is a phenomenal gift. The blessing is twofold. One, having a mother who is your best friend who has your back is really very important. And two, having a mother who is deeply rooted in her faith and her own sense of dignity.

GLORIA AND TERESA

Train up a child in the way he should go: and when he is old, he will not depart from it (Proverbs 22:6) Gloria would have never thought that her mother Teresa's seemingly cruel training would ultimately be helpful or that her own practices as a mother could be so wrongheaded. Gloria learned the hard way that a mother's "training" can be as significant as life and death.

GLORIA AND TERESA

Gloria's wears a sharp, and youthful haircut and has flawless skin that requires no makeup. She is forty-eight years old, but you'd never guess her age.   Like many women in her age group, she does have constant struggles with her weight. Her maturing body is perhaps the only indicator of her chronological age. Having given birth to two children, Gloria has seen her body change before. Gloria, a computer technician, returned to school to pursue her degree at the age of forty-one.   In spite of her extremely tough demeanor, she appears somewhat ill at ease as we begin our conversation about her life as Teresa's daughter.

Teresa was born in Alabama and being a very intelligent woman she was advanced in school and completed college at the age of nineteen. She worked as a principal, and later as a governess for a wealthy Ohio family. Subsequently, she and her husband relocated. They opened and owned a neighborhood convenience store and a food truck (restaurant on wheels) that sold hamburgers and other fast foods near the large city post office. Teresa primarily ran the store and had responsibility for her daughter and two sons. Her husband managed the mobile restaurant on the night shift.

"STICKS AND STONES MAY BREAK MY BONES BUT WORDS WILL NEVER HARM ME"

For most of her early childhood, Gloria had no indication that she had been adopted by Teresa. One day when she was twelve-years-old and always a curious child, she was rambling through her mother's "safe box." Among Teresa's important papers, Gloria found adoption papers for both herself and her brothers. Rather than being distraught, concerned or angry, Gloria thought that being adopted was a good thing and she excitedly proceeded to tell everyone in the neighborhood about her special status as an adopted child. When the news got back to Teresa, she was, as one might expect, quite upset. Perhaps today Gloria understands why Teresa was upset, but at the age of twelve, Teresa's anger was a mystery.

I thought it was something good. I went around the neighborhood telling everybody that I was adopted. I mean we were picked. When I had arguments with friends, I'd tell them, your mother had to have you but my mother picked me. I thought it was something special.

Gloria not only learned that she was adopted, but also that she had been born to an Italian woman who had other children. This knowledge helped to explain Gloria's very fair complexion and her fine brown hair. Throughout her childhood and as an adult, Gloria had little interest in seeking the identity of her biological mother. Those occasions when she was mildly curious, have been fleeting at best. She has wondered about the identity of her brothers and sisters, but has never taken any action to find them. As a young girl, she eventually had a brief encounter with her biological father who was African-American, but she never met nor sought to meet her biological mother.

You have those moments when you wonder, and then they're gone as fast as they came. You think about it for a minute and then you say, "what the hell.

"IF WORK WERE MEANT TO BE FUN, IT WOULD BE CALLED PLAY"

The childhood Gloria describes doesn't sound very much like a childhood. She was required to work each and every day in the family's store. Teresa was her day-to-day supervisor and was vigilant about Gloria being on task with various functions in the store. She was never allowed to play, and envied other children, including her brothers, who could leave school and go home to participate in child's play. Gloria was like Cinderella with two brothers who, in her eyes, were favored and pampered royalty. This favoritism was stark for Gloria, and even more so at around the age of eleven when her father, who treated her like a princess, suddenly died. A very difficult personal relationship with Teresa exacerbated the unhappiness of Gloria's childhood. They simply did not get along. Gloria cannot recall a time during her childhood when Teresa outwardly demonstrated love for her or told her that she loved her. Gloria is personally repulsed when she remembers the lengths she went to in order to try to gain Teresa's approval and love.

53

I always had to work. I worked when I was seven. Even though my mother and father owned a store, to pay our Catholic school tuition, we cleaned the classrooms. So when everybody else was eating lunch and having recess, we cleaned the cafeteria. After school, when everybody went home we cleaned the classrooms and that paid our tuition. When I came home, I had to work from the time I got out of school until ten o'clock at night when that truck left and the store closed. My brothers weren't requested to do this. I was. I didn't know any better. I thought this was a way of life. Get behind that counter; sell whatever had to be sold. Every night my father needed a bowl of chopped onions to go on the truck and my last duty every night was to cry and chop that bowl of onions. In between time, when it was slow, I did my homework. The other kids used to have so much fun, and I wanted to play, but I couldn't.

"KEEP YOUR DRESS DOWN AND YOUR PANTIES UP"

Being the only girl in the family, Gloria was always around the same males that spent time with her brothers. A tomboy of sorts, she didn't have girlfriends. She considered her brother's friends as her friends. She loved being around the fellas. They were all her buddies. There was one particular boy who was one of her brother's best friends and whom Teresa strongly favored. Gloria liked him too. Gloria's brother, attempting to gain favor with his best buddy, convinced her to have sex with him. One day while Teresa was away, with the support and encouragement of her brother, Gloria had sex in the basement of her home. She was only fifteen years old and really knew little of what sex was all about. As a matter of fact, Teresa had never even talked to Gloria about her menstrual. When it happened, she had simply told Gloria to go to the family store and get a box of Kotex off the shelf. Sometime later, Gloria recalls that Teresa, as intelligent and well-educated as she was, did explain things to her but did so in a exceedingly clinical manner.

That day in the basement, Teresa walked in and caught Gloria and her brother's best friend literally engaged in the sexual act. It was an ugly scene. After throwing this boy out of the house, Teresa, proceeded to angrily call Gloria a whore. This was not particularly upsetting to Gloria since Teresa frequently called her "slut" and "whore." She based this presumption on the fact that Gloria always hung around the guys. Gloria had sex only once with this young man and that encounter resulted in her becoming pregnant. She never considered marriage, abortion, or adoption. Gloria left Catholic school and attended a special school for pregnant girls. Later in the pregnancy, Teresa sent her to live with an Aunt in Alabama. At sixteen Gloria gave birth to a daughter, LaVette.

I went to school during the day and at night I went to work through almost the whole pregnancy. I left work going to have my baby. This was her punishment, to make me go to Alabama because she wanted to keep an eye on me. It was a difficult labor; it went on for a week. I wanted to go back to school and I wanted to work but that was a no, no. It was: I can't help you any longer.

Gloria had a second sexual encounter at the age of sixteen, that also resulted in a pregnancy and the birth of her son. Gloria did not leave Teresa's home until after her second child was born at the age of seventeen. This pregnancy was different for Gloria in several ways. First, Teresa did not know about it until very late in the pregnancy, and unlike with LaVette, Gloria received no pre-natal care. Also, unlike the difficult experience Gloria had with the delivery of LaVette, her son was a very easy birth. Perhaps the most significant difference was that Teresa had the baby taken away from Gloria and placed with an orphanage to be considered for adoption. It would be almost two years before Gloria could demonstrate that she could take care of her son and win the court battle for his custody.

When Gloria thinks of relationships and what Teresa taught her, she thinks of the way Teresa related so very differently to her brothers and of Teresa's views about men.

My mother was a totally take care of the man person. My father was a philanderer. He loved women. He would be out with women at night and I wondered how she could put up with it. She would always say, but he comes back home. I'm sure it mattered, but her thing was to do whatever your man said. Just as long as you're at home when he gets there. It was the same thing with the boys, just take care of them. It crippled them in life.

"THE LORD GAVE YOU FIVE SENSES, USE ALL SIX OF THEM"

Teresa also had a major influence on how Gloria approached motherhood and the relationship she sought to establish with her daughter, LaVette. Since Gloria had such a poor relationship with Teresa, she was determined that she would interact differently with LaVette. Gloria promised herself that she would always talk to her children, and she especially sought to develop a close and loving bond with LaVette. Gloria loved LaVette very much and as a young parent she did her best to provide well for her. Hard work was no issue. If Gloria knew how to do anything well, it was to work hard. Teresa had made sure of that. Often Gloria held two jobs in order to have enough money to care for her young family. They lived in nice places, and the children were always well-dressed. Gloria would discipline them, talk to them, help them with their homework, and attend the games, recitals and plays that they participated in. Unlike Teresa, Gloria wanted her daughter to have a "real" childhood, a childhood of laughter, fun, and play; the childhood that Gloria never had. She provided all the experiences that she had craved so much while growing up. Like going to the zoo or amusement parks and having big Christmas trees. She provided all that she thought went hand and glove with childhood. Play was a part of life for Gloria's children. Somehow, all of Gloria's care, hard work and good intentions did not change LaVette's course in life: a half-dozen abortions, two daughters out of wedlock, and an expensive cocaine habit.

I wasn't that much older than her, so she was unable to get by with things. She would get frustrated because I was always catching her. My daughter was something else. She would steal my car. She would sneak out at night without me knowing. Having an abortion didn't mean to her what it meant to me. She'd had five or six of them. I told her that she wasn't doing it anymore. I told her it was not a form of birth control. I had to explain that she was waiting too late. There was a heart beating,. The child was developed. I couldn't help her get rid of that.

Addressing LaVette's abortion problem was difficult but not nearly as difficult for Gloria as addressing her cocaine addiction. LaVette's cocaine habit initially created a distance between her and Gloria. Gloria did not know what LaVette was doing or where she was much of the time. LaVette, with two children, would leave home for days at a time. Gloria and Teresa would take care of her children. No one would know where to find her. Being streetwise, Gloria found her way to the various drug houses that LaVette frequented. She would often show up and remove LaVette in the midst of protest and whatever embarrassment her drug addicted daughter might have been capable of discerning. Eventually, Gloria came to know the dealers and others who were addicted. When they'd see her they would know that she was on the warpath looking for LaVette.

She would go away for two or three days and I would go and have to find her. I would go to the drug dealers' houses. I didn't care. I'd tell them that I know she's in there. If you don't send her out, I'll call the police and have them come in. They would put her out.

The pattern continued with LaVette and the drugs and with Gloria and Teresa caring for LaVette's children. Gloria needed a way to keep in touch with her daughter. She needed to keep communicating with her. As she pressed to try to get her to quit the drugs, Gloria saw the relationship and communication deteriorating and did not know what to do. Gloria reasoned naively that one way to bring her daughter closer and to stay on top of her lifestyle was to do what LaVette was doing. Gloria started to use drugs.

I had never done drugs before, and I was stupid. I didn't need to do it. I'm not going to blame it on her. It was the wrong way to keep in touch with her, but it was the way I did it. It's something I have to live with for the rest of my life. I was telling her to stop, quit, don't do it, and it was driving her away. Soon, I wasn't seeing her at all. I didn't have any communication with her. She was gone; I didn't know where she was and who she was with. That way she would let me in. I could find her at anytime. Maybe it was wrong, but that's what I did.

For a period of time Gloria and LaVette did drugs together and grew closer through their mutual involvement with cocaine. They knew the same people, spent time in some of the same places and generally hung out a lot together. At the age of twenty-four, LaVette died from an infection. The infection was masked in its diagnosis and treatment by her cocaine usage.

Today Gloria is a devoted grandmother who fights constant legal battles to maintain a relationship with her two granddaughters who are being raised by their father and paternal grandmother. The father, who never married LaVette and was her drug dealer, blames Gloria for LaVette's death and tries to keep her away from her granddaughters.

I never touched it again after she died. As easy as it came was as easy as it left. I just got up one morning and took all the paraphernalia, threw it out of the window, and never looked back. Got up the next morning and decided I was going back to school and enrolled in college. People wondered how I could just let go of the drug like that without going to a drug abuse clinic or something. I just concluded that I was doing it for a reason when I was doing it, and the reason wasn't there any longer.

When Gloria thinks about her life as a daughter, and of Teresa as a mother, it is not easy to find anything worthwhile that her mother provided. When probed, however, she realizes that it was due to Teresa that she has a strong work ethic and is able to take care of herself in this life journey. Gloria works extremely hard and is known by her employers and coworkers as someone who can be counted on to get the job done.

"BE CAREFUL HOW YOU TREAT PEOPLE ON THE WAY UP, THEY ARE THE SAME PEOPLE YOU MEET ON THE WAY DOWN"

Life has a way of taking its twists and turns, and sometimes even coming full circle. That was the case for Gloria and Teresa. Teresa lived to be eighty-nine-years- old eventually becoming very ill and unable to care for herself. It was Gloria, not her favored and pampered sons, who took charge of Teresa's care. She lived with Gloria for a couple of years as her health continued to decline. When Teresa reached the stage where she needed to be hospitalized for what seemed to Gloria an inhumane period of time and suffering, it was Gloria who would stop by Teresa's hospital bed every morning and every evening. It was Gloria who was known to all the nurses and doctors on every shift. It was Gloria who could make her mother laugh. Yet, today, five years after Teresa's death, Gloria remains unclear as to whether Teresa loved her.

She'd say I'm just proud of you, I'm so proud of you. But she's dying now, what are you proud of? That I'm here for you. I never felt like I was obligated to do it. I never felt resentment for doing it. I finally felt that she needed me, but I never felt that she loved me.

What could motivate a woman to care for someone she says never told her she loved her, stole her childhood, cursed her with regularity, rarely communicated with her and blatantly favored her brothers? For Gloria it is simple: *because she was my momma and I loved her.*

As LaVette's mother, Gloria shares the wisdom she hopes will benefit other mothers who are raising daughters.

Talk to your child. Give them the benefit of the doubt. Don't take your kid for granted. Be a mother. You can be a friend too, but keep your perspective. Be a mother first. Don't follow in my footsteps and be scared of losing your daughter. Find a way to help them deal with their problems instead of becoming a part of the problem. Don't take the easy way out by giving in. It may be hard, but find a solution to anything that is hurting or damaging your child, but find the right way to benefit both of you.

ELIZABETH AND MARGARET

Each of us is responsible for our own happiness. True happiness is found within. We will always be disappointed and unhappy if we seek to find happiness from someone else. Each of us has the potential for happiness because we have been blessed with the gift of life and the wonderful possibility of expressing the Spirit of God that is within us. Elizabeth learned about happiness from her observations of her mother Margaret. She believed that true happiness in life was embodied in a loving marital relationship. It took a lifetime for Elizabeth to understand that to find true happiness is not to find another to love, but to first truly love yourself.

ELIZABETH AND MARGARET

Elizabeth is seventy-two years old and though by no means showing wrinkles from her long life; her fair-skinned face glows with the wisdom, patience, and thoughtfulness of her years and experience. The vibrant colors and flair of her attire are excellent tell tale signs of her artistic bent. She is an accomplished artist and educator who has spent most of her life in the eastern part of the United States. Elizabeth is very precise and articulate when we talk very early on Sunday morning before she is to leave for the eight o'clock mass. Her mother, Margaret, also was an East Coast artist and educator, and the product of a family of well-educated African-American women dating back two generations. Margaret bore two daughters and a son. One daughter died in infancy. Elizabeth was Margaret's first-born child.

Elizabeth recalls a very rich childhood notwithstanding the fact that she grew up during the depression of the 1920s. Her focus, in recollecting her childhood, is not on the economic issues that her family faced during that period. Like most, the family struggled to make ends meet. Elizabeth's memories are rooted in the nurturing and caring environment that Margaret created for her family and the effort she undertook to assure a high quality of life. Within the context of the challenges represented during the depression, Margaret used her creative abilities to assist in providing the rich environment that Elizabeth recalls so vividly more than a half century later. It is as though one is being read a fairy tale when Elizabeth talks about Margaret and the circumstances of her youth.

Elizabeth remembers her mother happily singing songs and reciting ballads throughout the house while she would go about her daily chores. She remembers the joy of making toys out of orange crates and the beautiful clothes that Margaret made for her out of the better parts of worn sheets. She would make the clothes and then hand embroider and appliqué the old sheets creating lovely garments that Elizabeth proudly wore. She remembers always being surrounded with beautiful things and with feelings of warmth and caring. Elizabeth and Margaret did things together. Margaret often took her on outings for fun and learning. Elizabeth remembers her entire childhood feeling that she was in a wonderland of love and affection.

"NEVER FORGET FROM WHENCE YOU CAME"

Coming from a background of well-educated women, it is not surprising that Margaret stressed the critical importance of education. However, Margaret was somewhat unconventional in her thinking about how one should be educated. Margaret wanted Elizabeth to go beyond the rote learning of facts. She wanted Elizabeth to question, to think for herself, to use her own logic, and to be an individualist. Elizabeth was taught early that she could freely express her opinions and that she should not simply accept ideas and information because they were presented in books.

Elizabeth, like Margaret, was also creative. She expressed herself artistically and knew very early in life that she wanted to become an artist. When she graduated from a magnet high school for the arts and determined that she would continue her artistic training, Margaret's practical and protective nature interceded. After all of Elizabeth's training, and the role model Margaret had so ably provided, Elizabeth was stunned when Margaret resisted the idea of her pursuing a college degree in art.

I think I wanted to be an artist from the time I could breath. When I announced this half way through high school, my mother thought I was mad. That's when I heard that a Negro woman could not afford to go into a field like that. I said, no. I was going to get married and my husband was going to take care me. I could do whatever I wanted to do. She smiled sweetly. The saving grace was that mother's eldest sister was quite an accomplished artist, but she also taught. She said, "Margaret let her teach art. Let her teach it so she can feed herself."

Elizabeth remembers Margaret as a kind, soft and gentle person who was ahead of her time in her childrearing practices. She also remembers that she was a good disciplinarian who believed in and practiced physical punishment. Elizabeth would be spanked, but never felt that it was done in anger. The worst punishment for her was to see her mother's nose turn red and her eyes fill with tears. It was at those times that she truly knew she had done something wrong and that she had hurt her mother.

Every Easter my brother and I had new stuff, from the shining Mary Jane shoes and fancy socks, to a new dress and coat. I remember one Easter Sunday walking far away from our home to a church Easter parade. I still remember how I felt, thinking I really looked like hot stuff. I said to my brother, come on and walk back here with me. We don't want to walk next to mother. Mother had on a coat that she'd worn for years and she looked neat, but certainly didn't look as good as we looked. That's the spanking I remember. Every time that strap came down, I was reminded about how everything that I had and everything that I was had come because of her.

"WHAT YOU DON'T KNOW, DON'T HURT YOU"

Elizabeth recalls few discussions with Margaret on subjects surrounding her development as a woman. She graduated from high school at sixteen, and was always very bright and expressive. She could articulate ideas and concepts so well as to leave the impression that she understood, when in fact, she really didn't. This was the situation with Margaret and Elizabeth around the subject of her sexuality. Margaret, the epitome of an educator, supplied Elizabeth with reading material when she was asked questions about menstruation, having babies, or other things related to sexuality.

I said to my mother, what's Kotex for? She gave me a note in an envelope and told me to go and give it to the man in the bookstore. So I gave the envelope to the guy in the bookstore and he said, "Oh, I'm going to have to call your mother about this." He called her and she said yes it was okay to give me the book. The book was called Being Born. By the time I got home, I had read the entire book. It talked about the birds and the bees and how a man and a woman lay next to each other and make love. This is the way she handled stuff, the most professional educational way. I don't remember having direct conversations with her.

"WHEN DATING KEEP BOTH EYES OPEN, WHEN MARRIED CLOSE ONE"

Through her reading, Elizabeth developed the attitude that the sexual relationship between a man and woman was romantic and beautiful and she wondered why her friends considered it such a horrible act. Privately, she was somewhat embarrassed that this experience, which she viewed as so sensuous and inviting, could be talked about with such inhibition, mystery, and shame. When she married as a virgin bride, she carried with her an impermeable boundary between the fantasy and the reality of her sexuality, as well as an overall innocence about life in general. Even when she bore her daughter soon after her twentieth birthday, the experience was captured in the context of the total romanticism that surrounded Elizabeth's life.

> *I got married at nineteen. I barely, rarely dated. I actually believed when I got married that you couldn't have babies unless you were in love. I wanted to have my children naturally. She was born quite a bit prematurely. By the time they got me to the delivery room, she was here. Her birth was the singular most spiritual experience I've had in my life. I can remember feeling as if I was completely enveloped in light. I remember having a very strong consciousness of feeling part of the ultimate act of creation. I can still remember that feeling.*

Elizabeth's life as a child had been "storybook," and so too was her knowledge and expectation relative to the relationship between man and woman. Her parents were, in her estimation, the ideal couple. Although Margaret shared the childrearing responsibility with her husband, Elizabeth perceived her mother as really *running the show.* She recalls disagreements but not arguments, and silence but not shouting between her parents. Margaret and her husband would go for walks together and hold hands. He would often send her flowers. On occasion, as though he were still courting her, he would call her on the telephone and ask if he could take her out for a date. Sometimes they were so romantic in public, Elizabeth, even being a true romantic, would become embarrassed by their outward show of love and affection. This idyllic relationship was Elizabeth's model. She entered her marriage thinking that all men treated their wives this way and that her marriage would function similarly. She also entered marriage with a sense of dependency on her husband for his name, security and even her identity.

Elizabeth may have had an idealistic, romanticized view of marriage from the perspective of a child, but her reality was very different. Married life was a major struggle for Elizabeth. Although she was Catholic and divorce was not sanctioned, she eventually left her husband after thirteen years of marriage.

She doesn't like to talk about this period of her life, but it is evident that she experienced major personal and emotional pain. She felt totally unvalued in her relationship with her husband.

Following her divorce, Elizabeth essentially raised her daughter alone, trying desperately to protect her from the disappointments that her ex-husband had a tendency to cause, however infrequently he re-entered their lives. Regardless of her own personal pain, Elizabeth attempted to raise her daughter emphasizing that there was nothing other than God's love, more important than the love shared between man and woman. She wanted to protect her from knowing the harsh realities of life. For a period of time, she went as far as to create a romanticized version of her marriage so that her daughter would feel positively about her father and the possibility of loving relationships between men and women.

Love was everything. I was definitely a romantic. I believed I was going to look up to this man quite literally. He even had to be taller. I was going to defer to him in every way. It's amazing to me now. I was almost a clinging vine.

It was an extremely difficult marriage. It was an abusive marriage. It was mentally abusive. If it had not been for a priest I probably wouldn't be alive. If I didn't believe that there was a power beyond me I wouldn't be here now. I used to have some sort of childhood idea, that if you're good and you try to do everything right, then things are going to turn out right. That Alice and Wonderland thing turned into knowing the reality of how cruel life can be. I'm losing the most important thing, a marriage. I still feel that way at seventy-two. I don't have to be married, but I feel like there isn't a better state of life. That's still my little girl dream. If I met Mr. Right tomorrow, I'd marry.

"HE MIGHT NOT COME WHEN YOU WANT HIM, BUT HE'S ALWAYS ON TIME"

As Elizabeth gets older, she remains active and surrounds herself with people, especially younger people. Her aches and pains are minor and she continues to do all of the things she enjoys, only less. One of the most critical things that has happened to her as she has matured, is that she has strengthened her appreciation of her spirituality. She has come to understand that her relationship with God is her most critical relationship and she pays close attention to her spiritual connection.

As a mother, Elizabeth has raised her daughter in ways that resemble Margaret's practices. Her daughter is a well-educated artist and business woman who is forthright and expresses herself in a confident, self-assured manner. Like Margaret, Elizabeth has spoiled her daughter and made great sacrifices to provide her with what she needs in life.

Elizabeth credits Margaret with providing her with the strength to endure the trials in life and to bear the Christian burden of forgiveness and rising above unfair treatment. She has come to believe that if she equips herself with love for herself and for others that will provide the determination and will to overcome all odds.

I think aging is very, very exciting. I used to think that everything depended on me. Everything that I used to have as faith has turned into absolute knowledge of how God operates in my life. It's like climbing a mountain. The higher up I go, the more I see. The more I know, the more I realize I don't know. Possibility is infinite. I rely more on the spiritual side, on God. I don't have to have all the answers anymore. I wake up in the morning wondering what I am going to discover. I'm more relaxed. I'm more open. It's very exciting. It's like I'm getting younger instead of older.

My mother lived her life and she taught by what she was, how she lived, not by words. I learned things from her by her example. I learned strength from her when I don't even think she realized how strong she was. If I were giving advice to younger women, I would say to believe that you have everything that you need inside of your-self, if you connect yourself to that supreme power that's inside of you, which I call God, the Supreme Being.

RENEE AND OLIVE

It is natural as human beings that we do not want to lose the people we love. The possibly of the death of a loved one frightens us. Fear disappears when we realize that the spirits of those we love live on, and the love they have shared can live with us forever. Renee lost her mother, Olive, at a time when she needed her more than ever. Life's journey has helped Renee realize that death is a part of living. She has learned that the experience of loss can be strengthening and that a mother's love lives forever.

RENEE AND OLIVE

Renee is a single, forty-year-old social service professional working in a violent and economically depressed urban community. From her tranquil and generally cool-headed demeanor, it might be difficult to be convinced that she spends her days in the emotionally charged and complex world of providing consistent and quality services to young African-American women who are the victims of sexual assault. She is brown-skinned, short in stature and wears a short natural haircut. She greets me warmly. We engage in small talk during the brief drive to a location suitable for our conversation. Renee appears eager to share her life as Olive's daughter.

Olive was born and raised in Alabama and is the mother of Renee and one younger son. She was known to all who loved her as "Sister." Since she didn't marry until her mid thirties, she was also considered somewhat of a spinster. She bore, Renee, her first child, at the age of thirty-five. By this time, Olive had already established herself as quite a self-sufficient and self-supporting woman. Although Olive did not have a college degree, she had been raised by a very independent college-educated mother and carried that spirit in her life.

"WHEN IT RAINS, IT POURS"

Renee doesn't speak much of her childhood and growing up. She doesn't mention many of the things that are generally recalled about childhood, and the kinds of experiences that are typically internalized early in life. Renee does discuss her deep and sorrowful memories of losing loved ones. When Renee was only five years old, her father became ill with cancer. In order to alleviate Olive's burden of caring for a terminally-ill husband and two small children, Renee and her brother were sent out of state to live with their grandmother. This separation from Olive lasted two years until the death of Renee's father. As if the separation from Olive and the death of her father were not sufficient trauma for a young child, only one month following her father's death, her grandmother also died. This left Olive without a husband or a mother to assist her in carrying the weight of responsibility for two small children. Olive, just barely entering her fourth decade, was now alone and a widow confronted with being a single mother. With such tragic losses in her early years, it is no wonder that Renee's childhood brings back memories of loss, bereavement, and a sense of abandonment.

"YOU COME INTO THIS WORLD ALONE AND YOU WILL LEAVE THIS WORLD ALONE"

Olive was an excellent mother, and Renee could talk to her about anything and everything. She was a natural storyteller and often shared the vivid details of growing up in the south during the great depression of the 1920s. Renee felt a deep, intense closeness to Olive and she remembers clearly the messages delivered to her that influenced the direction of her decisions and life. Renee's earliest memories of Olive, as her primary female role model, are of a very strong, independent woman who worked hard and loved her children.

Olive made it crystal clear throughout Renee's life that it was of critical importance that she do and learn whatever was necessary to take care of herself. This included everything from learning to cook and sew, to training and educating herself for meaningful employment. Renee was taught early on to be independent. Olive did not want Renee to have to depend upon anyone, not even on her.

She instilled in me, that there was going to be a day when she wasn't going to be here. I remember her saying, "Now I want you to know how to do this because I'm not always going to be here to do it for you." It was almost like she had some sort of premonition.

Renee was taught the importance of learning and securing a quality education and was an excellent student throughout elementary and secondary school. When she graduated from high school, Olive was proud that her only daughter received a scholarship to attend a prestigious, private, liberal arts college. She was on her way to acquiring what she needed to be independent. Renee, too, was quite happy and was made plans for her life as a self-reliant, contemporary, professional woman. Then at nineteen-years-old, and at the end of her freshman year, Olive suddenly became ill and died. Renee, never having recovered from the loss of her father and grandmother, and still quite young, faced another shocking and unfortunate loss. If this were not enough tragedy, within three years following Olive's death, Renee's brother mysteriously disappeared. He totally distanced himself from the family out of shame and fear that they would not accept his homosexuality.

As Renee entered adulthood, and became a woman, she was without her grandmother, her father, her brother and mother—all the people that she had cherished most in her life. This circumstance was more than painful, it was heartbreaking. With Olive's independent nature deeply ingrained in her spirit, Renee continued college. Olive's sister became somewhat of a surrogate mother, but never came close to re-creating the relationship that Renee shared with Olive.

I think that it's only as I have gotten older that I really can appreciate the role she took on. She always made sure I had clothes and money. She did all the things that you need a parent to do. I can remember having some battles with her because I was trying to stake my independence. I think the confrontational phase I would have gone through with my mother; I went through with her. My mother is gone, and for some reason I internalized my mother's death to mean that I'm out here by myself. She had told me for so long, "Remember I'm not going to always be here." So I had been programmed to function very independently. Even today, it is very difficult for me to depend on people in certain ways. I was trained to be very independent.

Renee graduated from college and began to build her career. She has been quite successful, and Olive would likely be very proud that she has followed much of her advice and internalized so much of the wisdom that she attempted to provide. Like Olive, Renee's focus has been directed toward developing into an independent career woman. Like Olive who remained single until her mid thirties, Renee is now forty-years-old and single with no children.

Actually, you know, you just keep the pattern going. In a lot of ways I think I'm a lot like my mother around relationships, it's all that I know. She's the only model I had. I don't know if she could have really taught me anything else because she was so very independent.

Since Renee was so young when her father died, she doesn't recall very much about the love relationship between her parents. Although she has some memory of volatile arguments, Renee believes that they loved each other in their own ways. Olive did not live long enough to convey to Renee her wisdom about what to look for in a man or how to create a loving relationship.

She would say get your education, have your own bank account, and the other things that mothers tell you. But I think I internalized it so deeply that it takes a lot from me. It's like, okay now, to get into a relationship is it worth it, how much is it worth? For a long time I would just say, Oh, I don't want to get married, I don't need to get married. I'm just realizing, that was just something that was programmed into me. Now I'm getting in touch with who I am. As a result, I've put a lot of pressure on myself in the last eight years to try to find a husband. I really wish that I had known the role of male/female relationships, to understand what that union represents and why it is important. I'm acknowledging that I would like to have a significant other in my life. I've had relationships, but ultimately I pulled out of them real quick. Some of them were tied into abandonment issues, because when you lose parents, even a brother that you can't find, there's that fear of being close. I really wish that I'd had someone to tell me this, and not to have drummed in me that you had to be so independent. I've got to learn, and it's really difficult. It's difficult.

"YOU DON'T MISS THE WATER UNTIL THE WELL RUNS DRY"

Renee feels the deep loss of Olive even more as she grows older. She believes that this would be a time in her life when her mother could offer her tremendous support and direction around all kinds of issues and challenges that she is facing. Renee believes that had Olive lived, she would have been somewhat of a mirror in viewing her own life. She would, through viewing Olive's life from the eyes of a woman, have been able to evaluate and assess the impact of the things that Olive promoted about life. With that mirror, Renee might have realized that she didn't have to conduct her life in exactly the same way that Olive did. Renee also misses her mother as a person with whom she would have been able to share the ups and downs of life and growth. Between the ages of nineteen and forty, Renee has had many successes and high points as well as difficult decisions and disappointments. During these times she would have wanted to be in a position to turn to Olive.

As she matures, Renee also realizes that there were many important things about Olive that she never had an opportunity to learn. She doesn't know about Olive's aspirations, her dreams, her hopes, her pleasures and her disappointments in life. Spending most of her life without Olive, Renee has many unanswered questions about the woman who gave her life. She struggles and feels a void when it comes to a true understanding of this woman, Olive.

There are accomplishments that I am particularly proud of that I wish she had been here to see. I feel it deeply. There are certain things that I can recognize now that I missed, that I didn't know I missed. Somebody to tell you about relationships (and I am not so sure she would have been the best person tell me about that), but things that you need to know for preparation in life.

I have older women who I learned from just by observing. I learned from a lot from their mistakes. I would say, okay, I won't do that. I've made mistakes that may have been detrimental to my self-esteem. If I had just sat and talked with somebody, I might not have. That's another reason why having older women in my life has been important. Once I got past the period of being defiant and independent, I could really tune in and listen to them. Now, it's like, okay, now I'm listening. Growing is really a process, a hell of a process.

RACHEL AND SARAH

We must have the courage and the trust to remove our exterior masks and permit our loved ones to remove theirs. Only by going beneath the surface will we discover the beauty, truth, reality, and love that dwells within ourselves and others. Even under the most adverse circumstances, Rachel rarely saw her mother, Sarah, remove her external mask. Rachel learned how to mask her own feelings and viewed this skill as a sign of strength. She is now learning that you can't hide from yourself.

RACHEL AND SARAH

It is apparent from her weary appearance that Rachel, a fifty-six-year-old attorney, is tired. She has spent several twelve hour days in her office this week. She struggles to carry the heavy purse and bulging, overstuffed briefcase that remain her constant companions in spite of the terrible pain from recent lower back problems. She carries more body weight than she is accustomed to and more than her doctor has advised is healthy for her short, small frame. She has a youthful brown face and a short-cropped easy-care haircut with a few strands of gray intermingled in her natural curls. Rachel is the third generation of her family to reside in this large urban city in the Midwest. She is the second daughter of five children born to Sarah, a retired, second generation domestic worker.

Sarah is a petite, demur woman who is rarely seen without her impeccably applied makeup, wig and jewelry. Even at seventy-seven-years-old, she still has the flair, glamour, and radiant bright eyes of a much younger woman. Overall, she is active and in very good physical health, even better health than Rachel. Her only medically related issue is that she is in the early stages of Alzheimer's disease.

"WHAT'S GOOD FOR THE GOOSE IS GOOD FOR THE GANDER"

As a domestic worker, Sarah was frequently away from her own home. She routinely worked long hours tending to the household needs of wealthy suburban white families. Rachel somewhat resented Sarah's time away from home as well as the families that were, in her view, taking her mother away. What tempered Rachel's resentment was that these wealthy families often provided expensive clothes, shoes, and gifts for Sarah and her children who were living in almost abject poverty. Rachel would periodically be reminded of just how poor she really was when she would occasionally visit these homes with Sarah. She was astounded by the incredible wealth of her mother's employers. She learned early in life that not too far from her indigent surroundings there existed a different, materially rich world, and some families did not suffer through days of no heat, electricity, and little food.

Sarah wanted a better life for her children and stressed the importance of education. She never completed high school, but she realized that education was a way to escape the life of poverty and crime that her family knew so well. Rachel recalls fondly how Sarah would frequently read the newspaper to her with a touch of drama in every word, using a range of tones and inflections. It fascinated Rachel that Sarah could so easily breath such life to words. Rachel wanted to emulate Sarah and worked hard in school with the goal of one day being able to make words come to life like Sarah did. These early experiences shaped Rachel's desire to become a schoolteacher. She excelled in her academic pursuits and provided Sarah with great pride in her many accomplishments. Sarah would carry Rachel's report cards in her purse and proudly show anyone, especially her wealthy employers, how well her daughter performed in school. Her pride was just another motivator for Rachel to study and continue to excel. More than anything, Rachel wanted Sarah to be happy and proud of her success.

We wanted to strive to do the best job we could so that we could please our mother. She really, really instilled in us the need to relish getting a good education and make good of ourselves. She wanted all of us to be something and do something with our lives. She always talked about wanting to be an entertainer, wanting to be a dancer, and wanting to be a singer. She never really had an opportunity to explore it. So we wanted to do well in school to please her.

"EASY COME, EASY GO"

Rachel's father died when she was very young, and her stepfather was the only father figure she knew. Although Rachel loved him, he wasn't much of a paternal figure in that he was largely not accessible: as a well-known drug dealer, he spent the greater part of Rachel's childhood, in and out of prison. As such, Sarah was for all practical purposes a single parent. The family's circumstances would change during those brief interludes when Sarah's husband would complete a prison sentence and be released. He'd quickly reconnect with his drug business, get his cash flow going and begin to lavish on the family all the basic necessities of life that they couldn't ordinarily afford. His presence would mean good times. It was Christmas, no matter what time of year he showed up. It would not be long, however, before he'd get in trouble with the legal authorities and be gone again. The cycle of poverty would start anew. This pattern of intermittent incarceration continued throughout Rachel's childhood.

I can remember rather than going to church on Sunday, we would dress up and go and visit my stepfather. We knew a lot about prison life. I can remember as early as four, we would get all dolled up and go and sit on the front row of the courtroom. We would cry and fake tears so the judge would feel sorry for him and release him. We used to always write letters of appeal for my dad. When he was home for those short time periods because he was dealing in drugs. He had lots of cash. We would always eat well, live well. Then almost as quickly as he came home, he would be arrested again, and gone. We would have to go on welfare. I can remember putting cardboard in my shoes and in the winter, not having boots and a coat. We always lived in either a housing project or in some of the worst, dilapidated tenements.

"LOVE IS BLIND, YOU SEE WHAT YOU WANT TO SEE"

During Rachel's entire childhood, Sarah was completely loyal and devoted to her imprisoned husband. She didn't date nor have any involvement with other men even though years would pass without her husband being in the home. Rachel likens her mother to Corretta Scott King or Jacqueline Kennedy Onassis. She was both strong and regal in the most difficult times, and she presented to Rachel and the world, a face of strength, courage, and dignity, even as she struggled alone to raise her children. Rachel never saw Sarah cry or break down when her husband would be arrested and taken from the home. She always presented a stoic front for her daughters and a complete, steadfast allegiance to her husband. In somewhat of a romantic mode, she visited him religiously twice a week and wrote to him each and every day. She included him in every family activity by sending photographs and any other memorabilia that would keep him connected with the detail of the family's life. Rachel didn't see Sarah shed tears even when he was eventually violently murdered in an undercover drug bust.

"WHAT'S GOOD TO YOU MAY NOT BE WHAT'S GOOD FOR YOU"

As Rachel grew older, Sarah talked to her in somewhat general, euphemistic terms about her physical development as a woman and left unsaid the details of her sexuality. Poorly informed girlfriends and her older sister filled in the unspoken details on both matters. Rather than talk with Rachel about her body and the changes that were happening, Sarah stressed the notion of being "lady-like" and "proper" at all times. This rather chaste, virtuous notion seemed to Rachel too puritanical and prudish to accept in her fast-paced, inner-city world. Rachel, instead, wanted to be a part of the more wanton crowd and explore the off-limit areas that she knew her peers explored. Rachel's peers dismissed the sexual rules and conventions of their parents, and it was this norm that Rachel sought as her standard.

Rachel began to date a young man who was five years her senior. Being so poor, she thought that because he had a car and worked at the post office, that he was solidly middle class and ideal husband material. As an older man, he also seemed much more worldly, sophisticated, and informed about life. Rachel was impressed and thought he knew everything. When sex became an issue in their relationship, Rachel believed her seasoned sweetheart when he told her that a popular over-the-counter vaginal suppository would prevent pregnancy. She dated him throughout her high school years and for a time, their contraceptive technique appeared to work. Eventually their luck ran out, and by the time Rachel was seventeen and a high school senior, she was pregnant.

Sarah was disappointed that Rachel was pregnant and unmarried. She took the practical approach to the situation, by encouraging Rachel to get married. She provided a modest wedding reception, coached Rachel on how to camouflage her bulging six months with-child figure, and accepted the fact of her daughter's unfortunate circumstance. Sarah had to reconcile the fact that her daughters' lives were beginning to resemble the profile of most of the other young women in the community.

"LOVE IS A MENTAL DISEASE, IT DOESN'T RESPOND TO LOGIC"

Perhaps it was the combination of innocence and ignorance along with an acceptance of Sarah's idealized, romanticized view of life, that led Rachel to think of marriage as a Cinderella-like escape to paradise and her new husband as her "knight in shining armor." Following her marriage, Rachel left home and started life as a relatively naïve, uninformed bride and wife residing in the home of her in-laws. She completed high school and worked full-time while also attending junior college and raising her young daughter, Tracy. Life was rough for the newlywed mother. Sarah provided assistance by caring for her second granddaughter while Rachel maintained the hectic pace of work, school and wife.

Within a year, Rachel's knight in shining armor began to tarnish. Her middle class, idealized version of a husband was abusive and alcoholic. Unlike Sarah, who had so loyally stood with her drug-selling husband, Rachel left her spouse when she realized she had been wrong in her assessment of him. Without getting a divorce, she returned home with her infant child to live with Sarah. Rachel continued to work and to take courses in junior college. Because she was a serious student, eventually she was offered a scholarship and an opportunity to attend a four-year university. This was a dream come true and a Godfather offer that neither she nor Sarah could refuse. Sarah agreed to care for her grandchild full-time while Rachel left to attend college in a city some three hundred miles away.

Tracy would be six years old before the mother and daughter would reunite as a family unit. Tracy's resentment toward Rachel for leaving her began at this stage. She was mean and wanted to punish Rachel. Tracy wanted Rachel to feel guilty for leaving her and also for taking her away from her grandmother. Though the change brought an improved quality of life for Tracy, the improvements could not reverse what would become a lifelong rift between her and Rachel.

My mom raised Tracy. My mom had an opportunity to do for her the things that she had always wanted to do for us. She really lavished on her because she had time. She lavished her with love and adornment and everything. Tracy felt very special because of the way my mom treated her and raised her. But Tracy grew up being very resentful of me because she thought I had abandoned her. I always told her that I was going to come back when I graduated. When I did that, she actually did not want to go. She spent from about age eight until she was about twenty-two just really hating me, resisting me, and being very angry.

"You Have To Feed Some People With A Long Handled Spoon"

One of the most significant things that Sarah taught Rachel through her monogamous relationship with her incarcerated husband, was that loyalty was critical to relationships. Rachel deeply internalized this trait. The first evidence of this deep commitment to loyalty in Rachel's adult life was, although she left her husband after only one year of marriage, she did not divorce him until twelve years later. She would display this same behavior again in her second marriage. Today Rachel maintains a seventeen year exclusive relationship with a man who lives over a thousand miles away and whom she sees three or four times a year. Sarah instilled in Rachel the sense that relationships were treasures to be valued and maintained even under the most challenging circumstances.

She always felt that the most important quality, the most important aspect of a relationship, was loyalty. She was a romantic. She was a prude. She was very loyal. She ingrained those three characteristics in me. I wanted to be like her. I wanted my relationships to be those of loyalty and true love, the things I thought she was nurturing in her relationships.

Rachel's relationship with her daughter was not ideal. It was stormy. Tracy rejected and hated any man that came into Rachel's life. She was able to effectively position her father as the hero, and Rachel as the villain who had deserted the abusive alcoholic-turned-pious Black Muslim. She was especially resentful when Rachel decided to remarry a younger man. Rachel's second husband was unlike Tracy's father. He was more progressive, and understood Rachel's professional aspirations. Again, Rachel found herself in the position of being a romantic, starry-eyed woman who was simply madly in love. However, this time, like Sarah, Rachel had married a man involved in drugs. He was both as a user and a dealer. He had another trait that was unequivocally unacceptable to Sarah's daughter, he was not loyal. He betrayed Rachel time and again with numerous extramarital relationships. As she had done in her first marriage, Rachel was determined to be loyal and stuck with her womanizing husband for twelve years before getting a divorce.

It was just too painful. I really and truthfully loved him more than any man I've ever been involved with. But it was more pain than joy. We could never, ever see eye-to-eye on anything. He spent money and lived a very lavish lifestyle. I left him, but he wouldn't accept it. I knew that it was going to be very difficult for him to give up the fast lane and the fast life he was leading. He really lived and loved the beautiful life. The credit cards would always be up to the hilt. The rent was always due. The lights were on the verge of being cut off.

As Rachel grows older she sees more and more the nexus in her life and that of Sarah's. She is still the loyal romantic in her long distance relationship. Like Sarah wrote to her husband in prison each day, not a day goes by that Rachel does not communicate with her male friend. She sees him infrequently. Though he is by no means incarcerated in the criminal sense, he is imprisoned by personal and economic circumstances that limit his ability to be with her.

"To One To Whom Much Is Given, Much Is Required"

Rachel and Sarah have now lived together for the past seven years. Initially, they spent time traveling together as Rachel attempted to provide a life for Sarah that she had always dreamed of, but was never able to achieve. Rachel has taken over as the stoic, strong female leader of her extended family. As Sarah ages and experiences the onset of Alzheimer's disease, Rachel's role has become her mother's primary caretaker. She takes on total responsibility for addressing Sarah's needs. She makes great sacrifices in the quality of her own life. Rachel has also become the person that her siblings and their children turn to as the leader of the family. She is the one called upon to resolve the multiple issues that confront her large family, most of whom never escaped the poverty of Rachel's childhood. Her family has faced every serious issue imaginable including child and sexual abuse, drug selling and addiction, gang involvement, prostitution, HIV/AIDS, and criminal activity on all levels.

Now the roles are reversed. I used to look at my mom as being very tall and very stately. I've always seen her as being very beautiful, a lot more beautiful than I could ever be. I put her on a pedestal because she seemed to have worked so hard and somehow managed to take care of five kids alone. I really admired that. All I wanted to do when I grew up was to rescue my mother from this really hard life of scrubbing floors and working for rich families. I always wanted to take care of her because she was the one who had given me an opportunity to do the things that I never would have dreamed of. I am trying to take care of my mom. The relationship, at one point, really evolved to one of being friends. We became more like sisters rather than mother and daughter. She would actually call me and ask me for advice. The older I got, the more responsibility I took on in terms of being the matriarch of the family. Up until then, my mom really was the matriarch. I saw my mom struggling so hard trying to raise these niece's and nephew's kids, not really having the funds, really not having the kind of stamina that she had in the past. I so wanted her to have an easier life in her older years, and a life that was a lot more becoming of her. So I would always step in and try to solve all these problems.

With all of the difficulties and tragedies in her life, Sarah has continued to keep a strong exterior and Rachel has rarely seen her show outward emotion. She recalls two occasions during her entire life that Sarah allowed her feelings of pain and anguish to be exposed: once when she buried seven of her family members in a two-year period, and again when she learned that her only son was HIV positive.

I don't ever remember her breaking down and just crying. She would always say, "We're not going to cry. We're going to be very strong and get through this. We just have to pray." The first time I can actually say I saw my mom break down and cry was when my brother took us all out to dinner. He said he had something very important that he wanted to tell us. He said to all of us, "You know the reason I brought you out is so that I could break the news to you that I'm HIV positive and I just found out. I wanted to let you all know that it's not looking good right now." All of a sudden, out of nowhere, my mom just burst into tears and started crying, uncontrollably sobbing. That was really the first time I've ever, ever seen her in tears. She has ways maintained this very strong, silent exterior.

This incident was a saddening eye-opener for Rachel who for the first time saw her mother, always the epitome of strength and courage, as a frail, older woman in need of protection and support. Rachel saw a woman crumble in tears, who had always been capable of maintaining an air of complete external composure in all matter of internal suffering. Rachel also saw, on this occasion, an aspect of her own personality that Sarah had shaped. She realized that it had been many years since she had allowed herself to show any external signs of grief or sorrow. In her life, Rachel maintains a strong exterior in the midst of the very difficult and painful situations she confronts as the matriarch of her extended family. She describes it as a martyr complex, nurtured and modeled by Sarah. This complex causes her to constantly need to rescue even undeserving family members frequently at the risk of her own personal well-being and happiness.

I think about her death now mainly in the context of the Alzheimer's. I'm saddened and almost at the verge of saying that I really don't want her to have to go through this. If the only way she can be alive is to lose her memory, her persona, her personality, her mind, I'd rather she die an early death. I'd rather see her do that. The most painful part is her realization of what she's losing and her trying to hold on to a normal life. I know how difficult it is for her. I don't want her to die less of a human. I want her to be fully cognizant of who she is and what she is and how much she's given to people.

11

Rachel considers herself blessed with Sarah's strengths and hurt by her short-comings. She has developed a coping vehicle that allows her to experience extraordinary pain, traumatic situations, and catastrophic suffering, and yet not have it affect her outwardly. She displays for the world and for her family, the same Corretta Scott King and Jacqueline Kennedy Onassis exterior that she ascribes to Sarah. Rachel speaks with a sense of pride in her ability to be a poised observer and her capacity to emotionally step out of stressful situations finding a peaceful environment in her private cocoon. She doesn't relate her physical problems, including high blood pressure, debilitating back problems, nervous eating, and Lupus to her personal tragedies nor her body's manifestations of her life's hard knocks. She admits only that her ability to put a smile on her pain makes her that much more her mother's daughter.

So many times we take for granted the small things or the accomplishments that our moms have made, especially those of us, who are professionals. So many people take sole credit for their accomplishments and for everything obtained in life, not realizing that so much of it is a stepping stone from what your mom has been able to endure, and from what her mom has been able to endure. So much of who you are is a compilation of all those people and those women, especially black women. Our history is so tied into our future and our present and our children. I wish that she had taught me how to really be a lot tougher. Not on myself, but I sometimes feel that mom and I both are suckers. You tell us a sad story, or you reach out to us, and we are going to be there. So many of our family members have taken advantage of that characteristic that we both have.

KARLA AND EVA

Yesterday is gone forever. Tomorrow is not promised. Today is the best day to cast aside fear and distrust and begin to experience each new day with faith, trust and love.   For thirteen years, Karla kept a dark secret from her mother Eva. Only when she eventually shared her secret could she address her fears and distrust. She is beginning to understand that the secrets of our yesterdays are not sacred for our todays.

KARLA AND EVA

All around the neat apartment, there is evidence that Karla is closely connected to her African roots. The artwork, kente cloth swags as window treatments, and other accoutrements, all attest to her pride in this heritage. This connection and pride is more obvious when one observes the petite, twenty-nine-year-old mother of three young children with her hair fashioned in long "nubian locks." Karla smiles knowingly at the puzzled and confused look she receives when she says that she is a "naturalist hairstylist" by profession. She then explains that she works with natural products to enhance, nurture and cultivate the "original you." She is wearing fashionable coveralls, and on her small frame it is difficult to know that she is four months pregnant with her fourth child. She is the youngest of five children born to Eva. Eva is a fifty-year-old divorcee currently working in social work administration. Both women were born and raised in a large, urban northern city.

"God Takes Care Of Children And Fools"

Eva was a very protective, stay-at-home mom, who spent most of her time with her children. Eva gave Karla lots of attention, was affectionate and loving toward her. She allowed her to freely express her thoughts and feelings. Eva rarely allowed her children to venture far away from her with the exception of the time they spent with their paternal grandmother. This grandmother was special and was the favorite of everyone in the family. The children were not allowed to spend time alone in the home of Eva's mother. Eva was especially cautious in that situation because, at an early age, she had been sexually abused by her mother's best girlfriend. There was no way that she was

79

going to subject her children to such an environment. This experience had made Eva very wary and prudent in her decisions regarding in whose care she would entrust her children.

Karla describes her childhood as being *up in the sky*. As a young girl, she was somewhat of a contradiction, in that she was both a tomboy and a Miss Priss. She loved to run, climb trees, catch grasshoppers, and partake in other games that boys enjoyed. Conversely, she loved to dress up in frilly clothes and engage in girly, feminine activities. Karla had great fun as a child and felt a tremendous sense of freedom and independence.

Eva, having been an exceptional student, emphasized the importance of education. Although she had married young and started her family early, Eva had eventually managed to slowly complete both a bachelor's and a master's degree. She wanted the very best education for Karla, and she tried hard to teach her that it was important to have both *book smarts and street smarts*.

Eva was a young mother. Her exceptionally youthful appearance and attitude made Karla view her as not only a mother, but also as a friend. Additionally, mother and daughter shared several common characteristics that often fueled jealousy in the other children. Karla and Eva were the only two in the family who had darker skin. They were born under the same astrological sign and shared very similar personality traits. They were very close. Karla felt that she could talk about almost anything with Eva. Almost anything!

"THE SQUEAKY WHEEL GETS THE OIL"

Karla could not tell Eva that, beginning from the age of four, she had been sexually abused by an older male cousin. This cousin would frequently babysit for Eva and was always present when Karla would visit or spend the summer at the home of her paternal grandmother. The cousin lived with Karla's grandmother because his mother had been murdered when he was a toddler. Initially, his overtures were in the form of what Karla viewed as playful, innocent touching and fondling. Being so young, she thought the caressing and cuddling were loving behaviors and simple child's play. Since her cousin was very handsome and older, she looked up to and admired him. She even felt somewhat special in having his attention. Later, when he'd awaken her during the night and when the touching moved to more aggressive forms of sexual activity, Karla became uncomfortable and frightened. Though very young she began to realize that there was something terribly wrong with the entire experience. Still, she did not share this information with anyone.

For some reason, I still look back at why I wouldn't tell. I remember him saying that I would get in trouble. When you're young, you get in trouble for things. You don't always understand why you're getting in trouble. But I didn't have an adult mentality to try to process it. I just didn't want to get in trouble. Don't nobody want to get in trouble with their momma. My mother was my friend, but you don't want your friend to be upset with you about doing something. So that was how it was.

"WHAT'S DONE IN THE DARK WILL COME TO THE LIGHT"

Notwithstanding the fear of getting into trouble, Karla doesn't fully understand why she didn't tell Eva what was going on. Somehow, even upon reflection, there is the thought that their closeness should have overcome Karla's fears. She speculates that perhaps there is something that she may have forgotten or has psychologically blocked from her memory. Karla doesn't recall her exact age when she finally found the courage and trust to discuss her situation. Even then, she did not discuss it with Eva.

One time I did tell my grandmother. She talked to him and it never stopped. She was so in denial that it even happened, but at the same time she wanted to deal with it. She was so afraid that we wouldn't be able to come over there ever again. It was a lot for her. It was like an overload for her to have to deal with something of that nature. I remember her whipping him twice. I didn't know what was going on. I told grandma. Grandma is the head of the family. Nothing changed. I remember my uncle catching him messing with me, carrying me downstairs in the middle of the night. He tried to beat him up. He was so upset and grandma begged him not to tell. So, that kind of stuff confused me. It was like they ain't going to tell mom. She never told my mom.

The abuse went on for the next several years and so did the silence. No one told Eva that her daughter was being abused. She continued to feel that her children were safe with the grandmother that everyone viewed as the *greatest grandma in the world.* Karla continued to give the appearance of a happy, carefree child on the outside, while inside she harbored this huge secret. Because of her "special" relationship with her cousin, as early as age seven, she was beginning to learn about other adult experiences including drugs. Karla would hang around the teenagers, and she enjoyed the attention she'd receive from them. In addition to introducing her to drugs, they would take her to events and buy clothes for her. It really didn't matter very much what kind of attention Karla was getting. She simply felt good that these teenagers seemed to love her so much. Meanwhile, Eva assumed that Karla was in good hands with her teenage nieces and nephews. At the age of twelve, Karla was relieved when her cousin was arrested, jailed and later convicted of raping a young girl and a woman in the neighborhood. It would be five more years before Karla would tell Eva that she too, had been a victim. Karla would also learn that her sister was being abused.

When I told her she, couldn't believe it because she was always overprotective. That was the only place she would let us go freely. Grandmother was going to take care of you. Everybody loved my grandmother. Anybody would want this so-called grandmother. That was the one place that mom felt comfortable. She didn't feel comfortable letting me go anywhere else. I never remember her leaving me anywhere else.

"Love Can't Wait To Give, Lust Can't Wait To Get"

Karla entered her pubescent period already sexually scarred. She didn't trust adults in general because it had been adults who had left her so vulnerable to her cousin's abuse. She especially didn't trust the boys whose attention she was now beginning to attract. She wanted no parts of sex and any overtures in that direction met with immediate dismissal. Karla felt that intimate attractions were attempts to misuse her, and she would, without hesitation, extricate herself from the person or the situation. At the age of eighteen, and a senior in high school, feeling the pressure of her sexually active peers, Karla decided to have sex. Karla's early history of abuse was her benchmark for sexual encounters and as such, she was a passive partner. The physical act provided her with no pleasure. She really could do without this level of interaction in her relationships. Karla acknowledges that for a time she held a secret hatred for men because of what had been done to her. It was only later when she met the man who was to become her husband and the father of her children, that this hatred was uncovered and addressed.

Karla was fortunate to meet a man who cared about her and was sensitive to her feelings. With his love and support, as well as group counseling, Karla began to face the secrets of her past. She began to confront the guilt associated with thirteen years of keeping the secret of her molestation. She began the process of letting go of the hate she felt for all men and learning a different type of relationship through her husband.

It made me have issues with sex in general. If I thought someone wanted some, I don't care how much he bought me, how much he liked me, how much he shared with me or how much time we were together, I couldn't get along. My husband cared about how I felt. Anybody else, they just let you lay there. They're just trying to have sex and to get their rocks off. He was like, "No, this ain't what this is about. We're making love and you have to participate. You have to be involved and right now something is wrong. I want to know what's wrong before we continue." And I just started crying. For the first time, I knew that I didn't know how to have sex. No one ever taught me. At first I tried to fool him and say I'm in it. You know, playing my little orgasm moaning and stuff. That wasn't working. So for the first time, I knew he was different and cared about me. I knew I wanted to be with him for the rest of my life.

"EVERYONE MAKES MISTAKES, ONLY FOOLS REPEAT THEM"

While Karla was coming to grips with understanding and acknowledging her problems and many unresolved issues, Eva's strength was deteriorating. By the time Karla was seventeen years old, Eva had developed a serious addiction to cocaine.

I have seen my mom at the lowest point that a human being can be. I was living with her. You know, it was like she hit rock bottom. You know that they have their different priorities, not husband or children. I saw her deteriorate from being a mom and family woman, to just being out there. My mom went like mentally crazy. And I've seen her at the highest. She's recovering and getting back to the point where she went back to school and got her B.A. and M.A. So it's really a good feeling to see that because it lets you know how far you can go. I felt like I saw my mom be reborn. I really think she did well to have survived that. So now, I just look at my mom with such awe and greatness.

Karla never thought that any mother and daughter could be closer than she and Eva, but she believes that she has developed a similar level of closeness with her children. Her experiences as a daughter help her tremendously as she makes decisions as a mother. Through therapy and extensive reading, she continues to address the effects of her molestation, but she has fear for her children. She finds herself being overly protective, even more so than Eva.

It makes me overprotective. Like I said, I look back on my childhood and I was free. I'm climbing the roof and trees, running in everybody's house, playing, and doing whatever I wanted to do. But with my children, they've got to stay in the gate, got to stay on the porch, stay in the yard. They can't go hang out with my brothers. They can't hang out with my father-in-law. My father-in-law molested his daughter. It makes me uncomfortable for my daughter to be around my husband, any man, and any woman. It makes me suspicious. Because it was a woman who abused my mother. So I can't trust nobody. It just makes me want to give and instill in them as much as I can so that they will be able to communicate with me if anything like that happens. But I just couldn't see what would have happened to me to have told my mom.

I ain't ready for holding no more secrets. I held a secret for thirteen years. I ain't holding no more secrets. It destroyed things that could have been built, some healthy things that could have been built in my life. I don't know, sometimes it's a bad experience when it comes to dealing with my mate. Other than that, it was a good experience. It made me stronger and it made me a survivor. That's how I look at that.

VERNELL AND VERNELL

Life is not static. It has ebbs and flows, beginnings, endings and changes occurring all the time. Don't fear the changes in life. Know that there is nothing that you cannot handle with the unlimited expression of love. Vernell never loved her mother and the most they ever shared was that they were namesakes. With the living of life and the passing of time, Vernell has allowed herself to change. She is learning that love has the power to heal all wounds.

VERNELL AND VERNELL

Impeccably and conservatively dressed in a tailored pantsuit, this tall, fifty-ish woman with graying hair, gives an appearance of strength, sophistication, and savvy. She has a striking presence and you immediately perceive that she has her life under control. Vernell is a marketing manager and the oldest child and only daughter of Vernell. Yes, she is a junior, named after her mother. Mom, as Vernell refers to her mother, is seventy-nine years old. She married in her late teens and although she was basically a housewife, she was an extremely talented and creative woman who developed high-level skills as a seamstress and caterer. She taught her husband to sew, and the two of them would combine their talents to service weddings and parties. They would design and conceptualize everything involved for the occasion, ranging from the bridal gown and bridesmaid's dresses to the wedding cake. Mom was always very domestically oriented and loved to sew, cook, and everything that was considered the feminine home-loving role in her time. To this day, she loves dolls and her bedroom has a variety of them orderly arranged throughout. Family members tell the story that when Vernell was born she was treated like a live doll: pampered, dressed and played with as though she were a real living doll.

As the first born, and only girl, Vernell *ruled the roost*. She was always an independent child and this greatly frustrated Mom, who had a very strong need to be needed. While Vernell was self-assured and self-sufficient, her brother, born a year later, was the exact opposite. Everyone knew that he was Mom's favorite child because she was so obvious in the differential treatment she gave the two children. Vernell speculates that this favored status was because her brother needed Mom so much more than she did.

"NOTHING RUINS A DUCK LIKE ITS BILL"

Vernell has made a valiant effort to forget as much as possible of the detail surrounding her strained relationship with Mom. What she does remember definitely, is that they were never close. The distance between them developed early. The incident between Mom and Vernell that caused the critical breach in their relationship was an early betrayal of trust.

When I was about eight or nine years old, I shared something with my mother. I'm not sure exactly what it was, but it was a secret. I told her that this is just between you and me. She told her sister and her sister teased me about it. I vowed from that moment on that I would never tell my mother anything. I used to remember what it was that I told her. At one point it was so important to me. But it left such an impact on me that I made this decision in my mind that I wouldn't tell her anything ever again.

For very significant time periods during Vernell's childhood, Mom was not well. She suffered from long bouts of depression and had several nervous breakdowns. During those periods, Vernell and her father would take over the responsibilities associated with the maintenance of the household. Mom would be totally non-functional, uncommunicative, and isolated in her bedroom for very long periods of time. When Vernell was ten-years-old, her second brother was born. At this point, Vernell was old enough to more fully step up to the plate and take over during her mother's mental and emotional crises. Father and daughter, caught in this situation of care and responsibility for Mom and the family, were drawn closer to one another. Observing this closeness brought jealously from Mom, already a very emotionally vulnerable woman. Mom found ways to pay Vernell back for what she felt was a "them versus her" situation. Some of her behaviors were directed straight toward Vernell and were the kinds of things that children never forget and sometimes never forgive. Vernell still recalls her hurt when her Mom chose not to attend her elementary or high school graduations.

"THAT'S LIKE THE POT CALLING THE KETTLE BLACK"

Vernell unequivocally admits that she never loved her mother. She had little respect for her as a person or as a mother. She credited her only as someone that had given birth to her. Vernell spent a lot of time simply ignoring Mom and if she respected her at all, it was only because she held the title of mother.

Vernell criticized her mother's personal taste: *My mom liked real gaudy stuff. The more junk on it, the better she liked it. Actually, I used to be embarrassed about the way my mom dressed.*

She criticized her mother as a businesswoman: *People used to use her and they wouldn't pay her. She'd always put extra food and do all these things, and I would say, mom you're trying to run a business, you don't do that.*

She criticized her in general: *I always criticized what she did. The parts that I was criticizing were parts that she was doing wrong. I never complimented her on the parts that she was doing right. She was always trying to give me advice, and I'm like, please how would you know?*

"SELDOM VISITS MAKE LONGER FRIENDS, DON'T WEAR OUT WELCOME"

Not having the closeness of a relationship with her Mom, Vernell doesn't talk much about her mother's role in teaching her about her biological development as a woman. It is as though it just happened to her. She learned about menstruation from her father who had purchased books on the subject. He explained to Vernell what would happen to her body. Perhaps her cycle may have first occurred while her mother was emotionally unable to participate. In any case, Vernell didn't talk to her mother about this at all.

When Vernell thinks about coming of age as a woman, it is not focused on her physical development or psychological and emotional changes that she might have undergone. She discusses it in terms of gaining her independence from her mother. Their relationship was so distant and cold, so bitter and angry, that all Vernell could think about was when she would be able to leave home and escape from the mother she so hated.

Vernell was smart in school and was set to graduate a year early. This was perfect, in that she could now ready herself to leave home. At seventeen, she located and paid the advanced rent on an apartment. Gloating over the fact that she was now a woman and was getting away from Mom, she came home and announced that she was leaving. She was now positioned to act on Mom's constant threat that if she were so unhappy, then she could get out.

So I said cool, I'm out of here. I found the apartment. I had a job and I didn't want to go to college. I told my parents that I was leaving and that was the first time I ever saw my father cry. My mother tracked down the place, called, threatened, and told them that I was a minor and she would have them arrested for contributing to the delinquency of a minor. Anyway, the people called and told me that I couldn't have the apartment. I ended up having to stay at home. When I turned eighteen, I was gone. She told me that if you leave this house, don't ever come back, do not step across her threshold. I told her that this was my father's house too and I would come back to see him. I was not going back. I didn't care if I had to live in the streets. You don't want me back here, I'm not coming back, don't worry.

Vernell lived quite successfully independent of Mom. She landed a good job and was able to not only handle her rent but also bought furniture and a new Volkswagen. She also paid for her own vacations. She was having the time of her life. Several years of this lifestyle helped Vernell see that she needed to continue her education. She decided to go to college and left the city where her parents lived. Still, she tried her best not to come home spending even most summers on campus taking courses and working.

Vernell feels that having assumed so much responsibility at a young age is perhaps the primary reason she never married nor desired to have children. She felt as though she had already experienced that lifestyle during those lengthy periods when she'd take over during her mother's emotional instability. Her parents were married for fifty years, and though Vernell didn't understand how anyone could be happy living with Mom, she acknowledges that they had a good relationship. Although they would sometimes argue, the message Vernell ultimately received was that her parents were partners. It was definitely the two of them against the world.

I think he must have understood her. All my life I kept saying to myself, why does he put up with her? Why doesn't he just leave her? I didn't understand it. It didn't make sense to me. I just thought she was an evil, colored person. I never really knew her.

"ONE'S CHARACTER IS TESTED THROUGH BAD TIMES"

As an adult Vernell has seen clearer evidence of the love established in her Mom's marriage. When Mom was sixty-four she suffered a massive stroke and was confined to the intensive care unit for two months. She was not expected to live. Vernell's father was there for Mom again as he had been during her nervous breakdowns. He helped her relearn to walk and talk, and nursed her back to complete recovery. Mom's second stroke was devastating; and left her paralyzed and confined to a wheelchair. The marital relationship sustained this stroke as well, and Vernell's father continued to care for Mom, who was now totally incapacitated. One morning while getting dressed to take Mom out, Vernell's dad suddenly just keeled over and died. Fortunately, Mom was already in her wheelchair and could roll over to the phone. She called Vernell immediately.

She said, "Daddy's dead." How do you know he's dead, where is he? She said, "He's laying on the floor." Can you talk to him, is he saying anything, did he fall down? She said, "No, he's dead." I have a lot to thank God for because if she were in bed and he had dropped dead, they could have been in there alone for days.

Briefly following her father's death, Vernell's brother, who lived in the same state, placed Mom in a nursing home. At the time Vernell lived a thousand miles away and was unable to assist or take responsibility for making the decision regarding Mom's care. Some months later Vernell visited and was appalled by the poor conditions under which her mother was living and the overall state of her care and well-being. She moved Mom across the country to her home and for the past six years Vernell has been her sole caregiver. She receives no support from her brothers or sisters-in-law and hardly any financial support from other sources. Mom's condition has improved immensely under Vernell's doting and affectionate care. Despite her considerable improvement since being removed from the nursing home, Mom remains physically unable to do anything for herself and her short-term memory and cognitive abilities continue to decline. Vernell's challenges are awesome.

The challenges are financial: *When she was in a nursing home, she was allowed to be on Public Aid. They get three thousand dollars a month for her to get substandard care. When I brought her out they wouldn't give us a cent. She's not even eligible for Meals on Wheels. I'm feeling like I can't do it anymore. Taking care of her is a full-time job. I already have a full-time job to take care of her and to take care of me. We're not getting any money from anybody, anywhere. I have to work, otherwise, we are both on welfare.*

The challenges are professional: *I had a business trip a couple of weeks ago and I was just down to the wire. I said, I don't know what I'm going to do, I can't find somebody to come and stay with her overnight. I called this nursing home to find out if they had respite care. When I told her she was going to this place for a couple of days, she got ill. Her blood pressure shot up and she had a temperature. Then I got angry. I'm saying this is not fair to me. I have got to go to work and as her caregiver it's my responsibility to make sure that she is some place safe and cared for if I can't do it. She does not want to cooperate.*

The challenges are personal: *I have really come a long way from the day I brought my mom home. It's not anger; overwhelmed is the word. I am just constantly overwhelmed with everything that has to be done. I am a perfectionist. I want her to be cared for well. I personally have no life. I pray for Mondays, because there is a woman who comes in for three hours a day during the week. On the weekend, I am up to the plate all day by myself. It's just been a super challenge, the gyrations that I go through.*

"NOTHING BEATS A FAILURE LIKE A TRY"

For Vernell to try to find the wisdom from her life and relationship with her mother is a study of contrasts. The six years of caregiving that Vernell has provided have changed not only the quality of her mother's life, but the quality of the life they share. Mom now sees clearly who Vernell is in her life and the importance of having a loving and caring daughter. She tries hard to please Vernell and to show how much she loves and appreciates her. Every day when Vernell walks into Mom's room to begin the tasks of getting her prepared for the day, Mom greets her with a warm smile and tells her how beautiful she is. This means the world to Vernell. In her role of being "Mom to Mom," Vernell has finally begun to understand her mother. She has spent a lifetime viewing Mom as simply a biological vehicle and wrestling with resolving their differences. Through experience, she has found the love she has sought all of her life.

As a result of being a caregiver, I've seen some things that I didn't know before. Now that I've developed a relationship with her, I have to admit to myself that I can see some of the things perhaps my father liked. I'm even all weepy when I think about the decision to put her in a nursing home again. How am I going to feel not walking in her room every morning? She greets me saying, "Well good morning Ms. Sharpie, you look beautiful today." She tells me this almost everyday. I don't care how she feels; she could be in pain. Wow, how am I going to deal with that? We have come a really long way. I do love her. Either she's changed or I've changed, because the person I know now is not the person I thought I knew before. As recently as three years ago, I'd say she's my mother and it's my duty to do what I do. The Bible says Honor thy mother and thy father and that's what I'm doing. That's why this whole thing is so tough. Am I ready to let her go? That's what's going to happen if I put her in a nursing home. I've got to deal with my ability to let her go. I don't know. I just keep praying about it. I'm thinking, God why did you do this? I know that this has probably been a time for us to bond, but then all this is doing is making my life more difficult when she leaves.

ROSLYN AND ANNETTE

It is not only in biological conception that mother and daughter shape one another. Mothers give more than birth, and our bond with each other is strong and complex. Understanding that connection gives us the opportunity to love and value them for eternity. It doesn't take a long life for a mother to impact and influence her daughter. Roslyn didn't have the luxury of spending a lot of time with her mother, Annette. The early nurturing and wisdom Annette provided was sufficient for Roslyn to experience the benefits of the indelible mother/daughter bond.

ROSLYN AND ANNETTE

Roslyn has gone through considerable effort to accommodate our meeting on this gloomy, cloudy, afternoon. She left her office, took an extended lunch hour, drove several miles, and had difficulty finding parking. Consequently, when she finally settles in, it is imperative that she be given a moment to relax and unwind. The brief respite provides an opportunity to carefully observe the thirty-two-year-old manuscript editor. She is dressed in neatly pressed khaki slacks, with a white blouse belted in around her slim waist and tiny figure. She has reddish brown hair with a light complexion and wears no makeup. Her overall look is a tasteful, fashionable, preppy style. She has a confident air about her that is discernible both from her overall presence and her self-assured communication style. Roslyn is the oldest child and only daughter of the two children born to Annette. Annette, originally from Tennessee, was an elementary school teacher who later became a housewife and worked part-time as a tutor.

Roslyn spent her early childhood in a very middle class African-American community in the south. She grew up surrounded by successful, well-educated African-Americans and considered these models as the norm. Her own family history portrayed that model as well. The women from Roslyn's lineage who were college graduates spanned four generations. This history shaped both Annette's and Roslyn's perception and expectation that as African-American women, there were no boundaries to what they could achieve. Roslyn's early upbringing could be described as sheltered and somewhat bourgeois. Her identity as an African-American woman was shaped by positive successful images. Roslyn loved her life and enjoyed a happy childhood thriving in the protected environment of extended family and community. Roslyn was a self-described snob. She attended private schools, wore designer clothes, and fit in with everyone she typically encountered. Her comfort level changed dramatically at the age of eleven when Roslyn's family relocated to a small, predominately white college town in the Midwest.

"To Have A Friend, You Must First Be A Friend"

The move was traumatic for Roslyn, who found herself away from extended family and on the unfamiliar grounds of a community where she was a racial minority. Her emotional shock at the change was exacerbated because for the first time in her life, she was around African-Americans who were not middle class and who viewed her values as alien and suspect. Roslyn was quite naive and could not understand why she was having such a difficult time adapting. She didn't understand why her success orientation was viewed so negatively and why these African-Americans didn't share similar goals and standards.

Her classmates goaded and teased her, and she struggled with finding her place and identity within this new, smaller, more economically and educationally diverse African-American community. Her values and tastes were simply incompatible with those of many of her African-American peers. She couldn't understand why she wasn't accepted.

Annette struggled as well. She was no longer in close proximity to her family and the college classmates that comprised her extensive social network. In her opinion, the African-American social scene in this small midwestern community was not as highly developed, close-knit, or sophisticated as the one she had experienced all of her life. By the time Roslyn entered tenth grade, unwilling and perhaps unable to adjust her values, She chose her own path. She socially aligned herself with the white students. Although Roslyn clearly understood and acknowledged her identity and heritage as an African-American, her values, aspirations, and attitudes seemed more compatible with those of her white peers.

It was traumatic, in the sense that so much of my identity was and still is part of that earlier experience in the south. Once we moved, the meaning of being black was difficult for me. I expected white people not to know any better, but it really hurt me that black people were so crass. I had never experienced that. I never felt it was a problem because you spoke well, were well-dressed, had aspirations, or made good grades. Those were things that were good things. So I made a choice. If they can't deal with me as a black person, then I don't need them.

"YOU CAN TAKE A HORSE TO WATER, BUT YOU CAN'T MAKE HIM DRINK"

Annette was not concerned that Roslyn stood up for her beliefs and values, nor that she was at odds with her African-American peers. But she was concerned that Roslyn was ending up with virtually all white friends. She was particularly unsettled that when Roslyn began to date, most of her dates were white. Annette's strong southern orientation and solid African-American-based identity began to mount. She was quite direct in expressing her displeasure with Roslyn's decisions around interracial dating and questioned her about her lack of African-American friends in general. The intensity of her concern and her pressure increased as Roslyn grew older and began to mature physically and sexually.

At the age of sixteen, Roslyn decided that she no longer wanted to be a virgin. Being a product of the popular culture of the time, she had the attitude that it was expected, somewhat of a rite of passage, for a sixteen-year-old girl to lose her virginity. Roslyn was analytical and objective in making her decision on this matter. She had the benefit of sufficient sex education in school to understand the biological facts of her development. She also understood the practicality of taking proper precautions. Annette had discussed issues of sexuality with Roslyn and had provided her with a moral imperative to add to her analysis. Unfortunately, Annette had little credibility in this arena because she had informed Roslyn that she had experienced sex with only one partner, Roslyn's father. This acknowledgement provided more fuel for Roslyn's decision to pursue a sexual experience. She viewed Annette's declaration not as a romantic statement of innocent, committed love, but as a statement serving only to validate an inexperienced and outmoded point of view.

I had this very clinical detachment from sex, in as much as I didn't view this as an exchange of love. The guy I had sex with was not my boyfriend. He and I were just good friends. In some ways, I think I shortchanged myself. I didn't confuse having sexual desire with being in love with someone.

Roslyn could freely engage in conversation and discussion with Annette about matters related to sexuality, but she felt that their differences were so great that ultimately Annette's ideas bore little relevance in directing her behavior. When she was seventeen years old, Roslyn secretly obtained birth control pills, and after taking only her first dosage, she carelessly left the compact in open view in her bedroom. Annette found the birth control pills and immediately challenged Roslyn. As usual, Roslyn dealt with the issue in the intellectual, analytical, clinical manner that she approached matters of sexuality in general.

She just brought them to me and said, " What are these?" I was like, well you know the answer to that as well as I do. "Are you on the pill?" I said, mom I haven't even done anything, I've only taken one. She was very upset. My boyfriend, of course, was very embarrassed. I guess I didn't have sense enough to be. I just thought, a good offense is a strong defense.

Roslyn's matter-of-fact views about her sexuality extended to her uncharitable views on pregnancy. She felt that if women got pregnant, they were stupid. In her mind, there was absolutely no reason to become pregnant if you did not want to. She saw pregnancy as an end in itself never moving beyond to consider the fact that the end result of a pregnancy was the birth of a child. She held the stereotypical view that women became pregnant due to lack of access to information on how to avoid pregnancy. She hadn't considered that people do choose to bear children even when the pregnancy is unplanned. Annette tried to teach her a different view, one that considered the birth of a child as a gift as opposed to a punishment.

Annette's concern about Roslyn's lack of interaction with other African-American children accelerated when Roslyn began to consider attending college. Annette knew that the opportunity to redirect Roslyn's social life was either now or never. Her strategy was to find a way to get Roslyn excited about attending a historically black college or university. She decided to take Roslyn out of town to an annual football game between two African-American college teams. Attending this event with tens of thousands of African-Americans recalled for Roslyn her early life experiences in the South where she was surrounded by successful African-Americans. Her decision to attend college at this type of institution was immediate.

Roslyn left her small midwestern town to attend college in a much larger, more urban, city environment. Shortly thereafter, Annette became ill. Since Roslyn was away, she did not directly experience Annette's illness but she knew that it was critical. Annette suffered for what seemed to Roslyn, an incredibly long period of time. By the time Roslyn reached her nineteenth birthday, Annette was dead. This was an incredible loss for Roslyn because she was now at a period in her life and development as a woman when she needed Annette most.

It was really difficult for me because she was, like most women, sort of the glue that held us together. We were just getting to the point where we could move from that conflict age to really being friends. Right when that was about to happen, she died. I've spent a lot of time looking for these relationships with other people, reaching out to other people's mothers. I covet that.

"You're Never Too Old To Learn"

Not long after Annette's death, Roslyn began a four-year live-in relationship that eventually resulted in marriage. She has now been married for five years and is the proud mother of an infant son. Even though she lost her mother at a young age, Roslyn had sufficient time and interaction with Annette to directly obtain the critical wisdom, and indirectly, certain skills for developing a quality marital relationship.

She believed that you should be with somebody you love, who is your partner. She always wanted me to be with someone, a partner, with whom I could build a life, like she and my father had built together. I didn't grow up in a house where people fought, which I think has been problematic for me because I have a hard time expressing anger. I remember her saying never let anybody tell you your relationship is fifty-fifty. It's eighty-twenty; you're eighty and he's twenty. I also learned in watching her, how to work through things. Part of this goes against my feminist principles that you have to manage a man. At the same time, I do recognize that sometimes it's best to let him think it was his idea when it really wasn't.

Roslyn's father eventually remarried, and although Roslyn has an excellent relationship with both her stepmother and her mother-in-law, she is very different from both of them. This leaves Roslyn still somewhat positioned without a strong mother figure in her life. Ironically, the closest Roslyn has come to the identification of a mother/daughter relationship is with a paternal aunt. In developing this relationship, Roslyn feels that she is indirectly being guided by Annette's values because the aunt is someone Annette held in high regard.

Even though she is only thirty-two years old, Roslyn is quite cognizant of the changes that occur as women grow older. She's now a parent, experiencing the joys of motherhood and the obligation and responsibility of parenthood. She is in a marital relationship that, when the dating and live-in phases are included, extends to more than ten years. She is no longer the youngest person in her work setting and among her friends she has considerably more experience in dealing with life's issues. She sometimes misses the freedom and frivolity of being in her early twenties, hanging out, closing bars, and just generally having a carefree life. She is experiencing her womanhood by building a strong relationship with her husband and caring for her child.   She has also recently recovered from a medical crisis and now values her life and her health in a new way.

Like Annette, Roslyn has recently had to relocate from comfortable surrounding, leaving behind familiar places and people for a new and different environment. She thinks about how Annette must have felt moving from the south to the Midwest. She thinks about the sacrifices that Annette made for her family and this helps her manage her own transition more effectively. Roslyn finds that her childrearing practices mirror Annette's. She wants to establish a relationship with her child that reflects the type of respectful, yet open relationship that she had. Annette balanced the friend/mother relationship in a way that Roslyn considers critical, particularly in the raising of African-American children.   She is using this standard as her mothering model.

I feel like I've been married to this person for a really long time. Our relationship is very comfortable, not in the sense of complacent. We have a real rhythm together. He still makes me laugh all the time, and I still make him laugh. We have such a good time when we're together. I like this new kind of place we are in with the baby. He's so much more attractive with the baby. He's good at it. I like that we've grown together in that way. Relationships are really hard work, not just with a man, but also with friendship. I think love is being with people who help you to be your best but can accept the absolute worst in you.   You have to learn not to fear giving that to someone.   I think that's what life is all about. I feel like a lot of what I have to share with my mother, I can't ask her anymore. Part of me wishes that I could ask and really know. Other parts I know that I know from her. Just gaining more life experience as a woman allows me to have more insight into how she must have been feeling.

CAROLYNN AND TERESA

The lives of daughters and mothers are inescapably and intricately entwined and, like their genes, their love moves with us through generations. Carolynn was taught by her mother Teresa that mothers play the critical role in building a strong, loving family. Carolynn learned this lesson well and she is passing on to the next generation of daughters a family tradition of love.

CAROLYNN AND TERESA

Carolynn appears even more petite than she actually is as she gracefully glides through her large lakefront high-rise condominium filled with original art, family photographs and heirlooms. She's probably approaching sixty-years-old, but could easily be a decade younger. She is an attractive woman with straight brown hair, fair skin, and keen Anglo features. Carolynn is a widow, who took an early retirement from a successful administrative career in elementary and secondary education. She is the mother of a son and a daughter and the grandmother of two girls that she adores. Carolynn is the only daughter and the middle child of three children born to Teresa.

Teresa is eighty-three years old and spent most of her life in professional management positions with a government agency. While her children were growing up, she chose to stay at home and worked part-time as a welder during World War II.

Carolynn describes a childhood reminiscent of the type of family life so often portrayed in the situation comedies of the 1950s. She lived in a very small close-knit community, far away from the ills of the center of the large metropolitan area her community bordered. It was a working class environment with suburban qualities, that by today's standards would be described as very sheltered. Everyone knew each other and the young first-time homeowners worked hard to take care of their property and of each other.

Any responsible adult in the community could feel free to discipline Carolynn and neighbors were viewed much like extended family. The economic environment during the war was challenging, but Carolynn had no idea at the time the level of struggle that Teresa faced. Her childhood brings back thoughts of happiness, enjoyment, fun, playing, and a mother who was there for her under any and all circumstances. There were plenty of children who were allowed to freely romp and roam in the safety of this protected environment. Teresa never worried about the friendships and relationships that Carolynn developed because most likely these were the children of neighbors that she knew well, trusted, and respected. Childhood was a peaceful and somewhat idyllic time in Carolynn's life and she was very much unaware of the hardships and deprivation that existed not too far from where she lived.

Education was a high priority for Carolynn. Teresa stressed this from all conceivable directions. There was never any thought or discussion as to the inevitability that Carolynn would attend college. This was a must and a given. Teresa provided a rich learning environment in which reading and learning activities were as significant a part of Carolynn's life as play.

Teresa was a woman of substantial personal strength and was highly protective of her children. She valued individualism and encouraged Carolynn to assert herself freely and independently. Carolynn viewed Teresa as a woman who had no fears. She was someone who was bold when it came to standing up for her under any circumstance and with whomever she had to confront. She would challenge anyone when it came to assuring the safety and well-being of her family.

"PRETTY IS AS PRETTY DOES"

Carolynn was physically beautiful by most standards of her time. Teresa was careful to instill an understanding that there was far more to beauty than the outward appearance. She wanted Carolynn to learn as she had learned from her mother, that beauty was an inner quality that defined the behaviors and attitudes that people present in life. She was quick to dismiss the significance of the external qualities. Carolynn remembers that Teresa rarely wore any cosmetics, not even lipstick, needing neither to enhance her own natural beauty.

Pretty is as pretty does. My grandmother, mother, everybody would always say that. It's inner beauty that counts. Something can happen and outer beauty can be removed. You have inner beauty forever.

"IF YOU LIKE IT, I LOVE IT"

Carolynn was reared during a time when many mothers spoke very little about issues related to their physical maturation, especially when it had to do with sexuality. She never held any specific conversations with Teresa about the onset of her menstrual or what it would mean as she began to develop as a woman. These subjects were anathema and somewhat socially impolite material for open discussion. Carolynn learned about these matters, as most of her friends did, from books or from each other.

Even with such an innocent background and much to Teresa's dismay, while still in college, Carolynn decided to marry a man thirteen years her senior. When it became clear that Carolynn was not going to change her mind, Teresa did what she had always done and positioned herself in strong support of Carolynn and her decision. She stood by Carolynn as she sought to complete her college degree, even taking the responsibility of driving Carolynn to school each morning. Teresa's support for Carolynn never wavered. Carolynn was very much in love, and it was not long before Teresa fully accepted the early marriage. She totally embraced and supported the young couple. She was also at Carolynn's side, providing support and guidance, throughout her pregnancy with her first child. Teresa wanted only what she considered the best for Carolynn and taught her to recognize love and how to nurture and maintain a healthy relationship with her mate.

She ended up really loving my husband dearly, but initially he was still not good enough. I remember her telling me once, all the qualities she wanted this man I was going to marry to have. She wanted him to be well-rounded, well-bred, well educated. She wanted him to be handsome. She had all these very lofty qualities. She wanted him to have everything. She wanted him to have money, and she wanted me to have all the comforts, just everything you would ever want for your child. She wanted me to have the security of being with a person who loved me unconditionally.

"Don't Burn The Bridge That Brought You Over"

Carolynn was married for almost thirty years, and throughout that time, Teresa was supportive of her and her young family. When Carolynn's husband died suddenly, it was Teresa who was there with her providing the support she needed to carry on alone. Teresa even took the bold step of temporarily leaving her own home and husband to live with Carolynn to assure that she successfully made her adjustment and transition to life as a widow.

My children know that I'm in their corner. There is continuity among us. My children always knew that if I was not around, they could always go to my mother for whatever they needed. She was always there. I now watch my daughter with her children. She too is a tremendous mother. I'm just so pleased. She's very loving, very nurturing.

One of the most significant messages that Carolynn received from Teresa is that the family is our most critical social unit. Teresa was firm in her commitment to establishing and passing on family traditions. The entire family comes together often to celebrate holidays and other special occasions. They have customs and practices that have been passed on through the generations, dating back to Teresa's mother and her grandmother. Carolynn has completely embraced her role and responsibility for continuing these traditions.

"IF IT DOESN'T KILL YOU, IT WILL ONLY MAKE YOU STRONGER"

Teresa is now very ill, suffering from bone cancer and Carolynn is providing primary support. The strong medication takes its toll on Teresa's ability to function in the independent manner that she is accustomed to. The situation has been extremely difficult for both mother and daughter. It is difficult for Teresa to give up her self-sufficient way of life and it is difficult for Carolynn to observe her mother in such a weakened condition.

She has always managed. She's always been a very strong person. She never gave up on anything. That's why now it's so very hard to see her. It's like another person. It's very difficult. I think this is one of the hardest times of my life. Basically, I'm really trying to deal with this reversal of the roles. She's quite lucid, she's just unhappy. She wants to drive and she wants to be independent. She hates the fact that somebody has to stay in the house with her all the time, and that she doesn't have the privacy she used to have. I keep trying to talk to myself and stay strong and be positive. But, it's so hard.

Carolynn thinks often about her life and how Teresa raised her to value family and to be a strong and independent woman. She knows that it is Teresa's example that has carried her through this challenging phase of her life. Carolynn frequently contemplates the fact that she is a member of a generation of daughters who are seeing their mothers live longer. She understands that she is coping with Teresa's decline with little or no emotional and psychological preparation. She knows that this is a new role and as tradition would have it, her daughter is watching the process carefully. Carolynn believes that her daughter, now thirty-six years old, will be better equipped because she has seen first-hand how Carolynn has provided support for Teresa. They talk about this subject and see the natural preparation of moving to the next generation of mother/daughter relationship. Carolynn's wisdom for life from Teresa, and now, Carolynn's wisdom to her daughter is the same.

Tradition has been so important to me. Love your family, that's foremost. You just stay in there. You just stay strong.

LEILA, MARY AND NANCY

Before we can fully love another, we must heal our own wounds. This means that we must acknowledge and accept our past, no matter how troubling or painful. Then we must work through it.   For half of her life, Leila felt rejection because she was raised by Mary instead of by her biological mother Nancy. Leila was left with deep wounds and finds it difficult to acknowledge and accept her past. She knows that if she does not make peace with her history she will continue to spend every-day reliving her pain.

LEILA, MARY AND NANCY

Leila's anxiousness to talk is evident when she arrives almost half an hour early on this Saturday morning.   As she enters, she fills the height of the door. She is strikingly tall, standing over six feet and though a very large woman, carries herself in a dainty, elegant manner. She has beautiful, smooth, flawless dark-caramel colored skin, and a face that could grace the cover of a beauty magazine. She is neatly dressed, wearing denim jeans and a sweater and her hair is woven with shoulder-length auburn curls.

Leila is a thirty-one-year-old social worker from a small town in Virginia. She was raised as the only daughter of Mary, a housewife and a non-professional state employee. Mary is not Leila's biological mother though there is a blood relationship between them. Mary is Leila's aunt, the sister of Nancy who is her biological mother.

When Nancy was twenty-three years old and a pregnant graduate student, her marriage fell apart and she found herself divorced and alone with her infant daughter, Leila. Nancy brought her child home and gave the baby to her sister, Mary, to raise as her own. Nancy then returned to school to continue her education leaving Leila to be raised as Mary's daughter.

I guess I didn't fit into the picture. She brought me home to Virginia and I was raised by my aunt and uncle, who I refer to as my parents. And that's where the story begins, as we say.

"FEELINGS ARE FACTS, PAY ATTENTION TO THEM"

Growing up in a small country-town carried with it all of the stereotypical mental pictures that one might imagine. There was little activity or other diversions for Leila. Her childhood was lacking in richness in terms of exposure to a range of quality social and educational experiences. In Leila's perception, the people around her led rather average and mundane lifestyles. They seemed limited in their hopes and aspirations. Everyone was familiar with each other's lives, and Leila lived within walking distance of an array of relatives, including her grandparents. Leila always knew that there was something about her that was different from her family members. Her physical appearance was so starkly different from Mary's that she knew very early and somewhat instinctively, that there was something unusual. Leila was still quite young when she figured out that the cloud of difference she felt had to do with the fact that she was not Mary's child. Although it was never stated, she knew that the woman that she called mother was really her aunt.

Living in an extended family environment, Leila would often have occasion to interface with her mother/aunt, Nancy. There was a striking resemblance between the two, with both having distinctive physical qualities dissimilar to most of the other family members. When Nancy visited the family, she treated Leila as her niece, even though everyone, including Leila, knew that she was actually her mother.

I never really had a relationship with my biological mother. She played the role in my life as being an aunt. I would naturally avoid her on purpose. Growing up, I had a lot of anger toward her because basically she denied who I was. It was difficult having someone who you know is your mother act like you don't exist as their child and recognize you as just being another relative.

"MONEY CAN'T BUY HAPPINESS"

This type of relationship continued throughout Leila's childhood. Nancy would visit and would show no special love or connection to Leila. Leila's anger and resentment grew with every encounter. When Nancy remarried and started a family with her new husband, Leila's pain intensified. The family visits became more complicated when Leila would be placed in the position of interaction with her siblings/cousins. It hurt Leila more as she observed the quality of life that Nancy had established for herself and her " new" family. Nancy had completed her doctorate degree and was doing quite well economically. Her lifestyle was on a far higher scale than the simple, country life that Leila was leading as Mary's daughter. Leila was keenly aware of the love that Nancy gave to her other children, the material possessions, and the overall quality of the lifestyle that they were leading. She couldn't help but envy her siblings/cousins living a life that she felt also belonged to her.

"Never Ruin An Apology With An Excuse"

Leila's anger with Nancy was intense but unspoken, since the subject of her background was the epitome of a family *skeleton in the closet*. Leila never shared her feelings and emotions about her identity. She did not want to hurt Mary, who was a good mother and working hard to raise her in the best way that she knew how. She couldn't talk to her grandparents because Nancy was their favorite, most successful child and held a special position in the family. The only person left to address was Nancy.

While visiting an out-of-town aunt who lived near Nancy, Leila decided to confront her. Leila's memory of this confrontation is as fresh as if the event occurred yesterday. She was fifteen-years-old that summer when she decided to ask Nancy about the circumstances of her birth. She was totally discouraged and disheartened when Nancy denied that she was indeed her mother. Nancy told Leila that she was an illegitimate child that her ex-husband had brought home for her to raise. She informed Leila that when they divorced, she asked Mary to raise the child. Further, Nancy told Leila that she should consider it a favor and be thankful that she had identified a good family to raise her. Leila was devastated by the tale that Nancy had woven. She also lost complete respect for her as both a woman and as a mother. From that point forward, Leila has had basically no communication with her biological mother and the wrenching distance between them appears impenetrable. Like there was no affirmation from Nancy as mother, there is now no affirmation from Leila as her daughter.

We never talked about emotions, feelings, and stuff like that. Imagine what it is like as a child with all these emotions and feelings going on but you can't talk about them with anyone.

"Never Mix Forgiveness With Blame"

Leila's anger and resentment toward Nancy were intense enough to serve as a strong motivating force for her to do well in school. She wanted to assure that she could make a better life for herself than the life Nancy had relegated to her. All the while, however, it remained the family's (known to everyone) secret, that Nancy was really Leila's mother. Consequently, Leila grew up with acute identity issues.

Everybody knew it. No one would actually come out verbally and say it, but it was known. So we all pretended. I grew up knowing that I was different. I wouldn't say that I had a happy childhood. I had issues just trying to figure out who I was. I did not fit in, and I couldn't wait to get out.

Throughout Leila's youth, the family lived the lie of her birth. Mary was a good mother, raising Leila apparently without any compensation or support from Nancy. She raised Leila with a strong value toward education and Nancy modeled from a distance, the type of lifestyle that could be attained with a good educational background. Leila bought into this value system. She saw the good life that Nancy was leading, and she also viewed education as a means of escape from the country town that was her home. She also needed a vehicle to remove herself from a circumstance that made her feel as though she didn't belong and where she felt incredibly different from everyone around her. She knew that a whole new world existed for her to explore and education was the key.

Leila loved Mary and she felt that she was loved. She does, however, criticize Mary's parenting. Mary worked a lot, and Leila was often left alone and unsupervised in the company of older male cousins. As a "different" child, her cousins subjected her to sexual abuse as early as the age of eight. Leila did not share this with Mary. By this time, her feelings of being "different" were so strong that she had internalized a notion that bad things were just meant to happen to her. She believed that it was her fault. The sexual violations continued until she was old enough to be able to stop them herself.

Leila managed to complete high school and left the country town to attend college. Her real goal, however, was to escape the life that she so hated. She carried with her questions of her individual identity and worth, an intense anger toward Nancy and a fearfulness about the abusiveness of men. Through most of her college experience, Leila avoided sexual relationships with men. She didn't have boyfriends and almost completely isolated herself from any type of romantic relationship. Given her early experiences, sex was not something that she viewed positively. Although most of her peers were sexually active, Leila did not have her first voluntary sexual experience until she was twenty years old. It took a study abroad program and the positive attention she received as an American on foreign soil, to allow her to feel a level of self-esteem sufficient to engage in an intimate, sexual relationship. Even today, the anger Leila harbors toward Nancy and the early sexual abuse interfere with her ability to function in an intimate relationship.

For some reason, being denied something that I was entitled to, has made intimacy hard for me. It's easy to be intimate and very generous and loving to children in my work. I see them as being very vulnerable. But I've sabotaged a lot of my adult relationships. That's unconscious, but at any rate I've never had that maternal figure, that gives you the wisdom and the role model of how to handle these situations.

"YOU HAVE TO PLAY THE HAND YOU'RE DEALT"

Leila is by most definitions a professionally successful woman. She loves her work and the positive impact that she can have on the lives of troubled children. She is somewhat of a workaholic and her deep commitment to the children serves to compensate for the voids in her life. She is frequently positioned to provide advice and guidance to young women who have had childhood experiences similar to her own. Ironically, in these instances, Leila's strong advice is that her clients resolve issues early in life. She tells these young women how damaging it is to carry forward the pain and anger of childhood into adult life. She tells them that being in foster care and adoptive situations, does not mean that they are incapable of loving and being loved. Leila, aware of the hypocrisy, tells these young women to do everything that she should do and has not done in her life.

In many ways Leila acknowledges that she is very much like her mother and this fact has loomed large over her development. She, like Nancy, pursued her education and her career at some sacrifice to her personal life. She considers her career as the most important aspect of her life and defines herself within that context. Like Nancy, Leila has also placed her career ahead of becoming a parent. When she was twenty-eight-years-old and in the midst of completing her master's degree, Leila learned that she was pregnant. When she reluctantly speaks to her reasons for aborting the pregnancy, after an uncomfortably long period of silence, her words sound much like those she uses to describe why Nancy gave her to Mary.

I've never talked about it. It happened and I dealt with it at the time. I had made a mistake. I got an abortion and that's it. I made a conscious choice that parenting was not on the agenda. I was not prepared for it and I didn't want to be a single mother. I wasn't ready and I did something about it. Like I said, children weren't in the plan at the time.

Leila continues unsuccessfully to try to address her anger toward Nancy. She has sought counseling and is quite adept at articulating the psychological terminology that describes her current emotional state. At thirty-one, she feels that she has built an identity for herself that she never had with either Mary or Nancy. She has spent more than one half of her life seeking this definition of herself. As she moves forward in her life journey, Leila knows that she must ultimately address her anger and face all the secrets and silence she has kept. She is intelligent enough to realize that the walls she has built around herself cannot protect and shield her from the intense feelings she has inside. She knows that to truly find inner peace, she must shed the anger and begin to understand, accept, appreciate, and love herself.

It's something that my life is so much like Nancy's, the very person that I don't want to be like. I've had all this anger. I've tried so hard not to be like her. I've tried so hard to deny anything that I am that is like her. I try to deny that she made me motivated, ambitious and made me know that I could succeed. I can't deny that I have her genetics. In some twisted sense, I'm turning out to be what I've always wanted not to be, which is her.

RHONDA AND MARGARET

Treasure every life experience that God gives to you and consider the lessons and blessings that each of these experiences provide. Each moment we live is an integral component of the YOU that is forever becoming. Alzheimer's disease has required Rhonda to become mother to her mother, Margaret. Not only is she mothering her mother, but when she examines herself closely, she sees that the YOU she is becoming is her mother.

RHONDA AND MARGARET

On the evening we met for the first time, there was an immediate comfort level and one would have assumed that we had known each other for a life-time. Rhonda was warm, friendly and relaxed. She shared an engaging smile that brightened an already twelve-hour workday. In contrast to my jeans, the forty-plus-year-old Rhonda, was clearly attired for something special. She was wearing her hair in small, neatly braided cornrows with long extensions, and a loose-fitting Caftan-type dress. Rhonda proudly described herself as having three careers: computer instructor, sales representative and vocalist. Her singing voice is a cross between Cassandra Wilson and Roberta Flack, and her presence reflects the best of both. She has brought her teenage son along with her and we quickly dispatch him to another room so that we can talk freely and candidly about her and and her mother Margaret.

Margaret, at eighty-one-years-old, is a retired registered nurse. She is origi-nally from Georgia. She bore four children, with Rhonda being the younger of the two girls. She is a proud grandmother of many of which three belong to Rhonda. Soft spoken but well-recognized best describes Margaret. Rather like the phrase usually reserved for men, Rhonda calls Margaret, *the strong, silent type.* Although Margaret was a leader in church and in school organizations, she managed to have a powerful influence without being center stage. Rhonda learned this quality well and is calm and somewhat low-key in her style. Still, she clearly positions herself from a base of strength and courage.

There has always been somewhat of an indelible bond between Rhonda and Margaret. One of the earliest indicators of this attachment was exhibited in a serious case of eczema that initially flared up in Rhonda when Margaret returned to work full-time two weeks following her birth. As long as Margaret continued to be employed full-time, Rhonda's eczema remained quite serious.

"STRIVE TO REACH THE TOP BECAUSE IT'S CROWDED AT THE BOTTOM"

As an educated woman, Margaret stressed not only the importance of education, but also more specifically, the absolute necessity that Rhonda should receive a college degree. School and education, along with church and faith, were her unquestioned priorities. She not only "talked the talk" but she "walked the walk." She demonstrated her commitment by actively involving herself in the education of her children and making church attendance and participation a part of her family's life. In the school system, Rhonda had little leeway for distraction because Margaret was well-known and involved at every level. She served inside the school as a school/community representative and at home helped Rhonda with homework and extracurricular activities. Even though she worked private duty nursing at night, she managed her maternal responsibilities as though she were a full-time housewife and mother. Margaret always had lunch prepared when her children came home and required that they all eat the evening meal as a family. It seemed to Rhonda that Margaret was everywhere. She doesn't remember her ever sleeping.

"TALK SLOWLY, BUT THINK QUICKLY"

In her early years, Rhonda viewed Margaret as a loving and giving mother but not as someone who was easy to communicate with. She wouldn't open up when Rhonda would try to engage her on a one-to-one level. It seemed to Rhonda that she was closed and unable to share of her inner feelings. Although there are many fond memories of all the good domestic things that Margaret did, Rhonda felt a void and a distance when it came to talking to her mother. In spite of these rather warm familial scenes that Rhonda remembers so well, as an adult, Rhonda describes her family as dysfunctional.

I didn't know I was from a dysfunctional family until my adulthood. The term dysfunctional is used in that my mother stayed in the marriage because of the children. A lot of these things weren't revealed to me until later. My father overcame a gambling disease so she struggled, but she made it. She later shared with me how she struggled and always reminded me that I didn't have to do that.

Rhonda and Margaret's relationship, though basically pleasant during childhood, changed toward the negative as Rhonda became a teenager and young woman. Margaret's inability to communicate effectively worsened the natural rift that develops between mother and daughter during the awkward pubescent period. Rhonda wanted to grow up faster than Margaret wanted her to. With a sister who was about ten years older, it was easy for Rhonda to slip into a role that was more mature than her chronological years.

Although generally short on expressions of feelings, as a nurse, Margaret was adept in her ability to communicate with Rhonda regarding her sexual maturation. These are conversations that Rhonda vividly recalls because of the positive way Margaret positioned the process and all of the wonderful changes that were in store for her. Margaret talked candidly about the beauty and power inherent in a woman's body and her ability to give birth. Although Rhonda experienced very painful menstrual cycles, she was never taught that this experience was anything other than a beautiful, natural, womanly occurrence. Margaret was so sensitive to Rhonda that she would literally shed tears when Rhonda had her painful monthly period. This was not considered or conveyed as a curse or an unclean, shameful, monthly taboo, but as a very natural part of womanhood. Margaret was also a realist when it came to raising a daughter. Rhonda hated the fact that she had to show her the used sanitary napkins. Margaret would tell Rhonda that she was only insisting upon this practice to assure that the cycle was okay and that there were no issues that needed her attention. It wasn't long before Rhonda figured out that Margaret's real agenda, was to make sure she was not pregnant.

Even though Margaret was very frank and straightforward around the subject of sexuality, Rhonda felt it necessary to hide her sexual experimentation. This was a part of her growth that she just didn't feel comfortable sharing with Margaret. Although her older sister and an older cousin tried vainly to open communication on the subject, Rhonda did not expose herself, ultimately turning to her less informed peers for advice. At sixteen, following her first sexual encounter, she was pregnant. It was not until she miscarried that Margaret learned that her youngest daughter was sexually active.

It hurt her. I think the most important thing to her was how her reputation was at stake and that I didn't open up. I've always said that I hope I don't have that problem with my daughter. I don't why know why I never felt comfortable talking about it.

After the miscarriage, Margaret took Rhonda to the doctor and immediately became more proactive by placing her on birth control pills. Rhonda, having had the misfortune of getting pregnant on her first experience with sexual intercourse, objected strenuously. She told Margaret that she was no longer engaging in sex. The doctor had already made Rhonda feel dirty and promiscuous. Margaret made the situation worse by insisting that she take the birth control pills. Later, both Margaret and Rhonda would position her use of contraceptives as a purposeful medical action to provide relief from her monthly agony with menstrual cramps.

Rhonda's daughter is now sixteen and Rhonda has been trying to break the ice with her and encourage her to share. But like Rhonda was with Margaret, Alyse won't open up other than to assure Rhonda that there is nothing to share. Rhonda understands how this could happen, since it is happening to her, as a mother, almost exactly as it did with Margaret.

> *She's a very attractive girl. She's an athlete so she's around young men all the time. I know that my perception of my mother when I was a child was that, she didn't know what it was about anyway. I had this perception that mom wouldn't understand. Now I am where she was.*

"NEVER PUT A PERIOD WHERE A COMMA OUGHT TO BE"

Rhonda didn't marry and have her first child until she was in her mid twenties. As a young college graduate her relationship with Margaret began to grow into an open, honest, woman to woman connection. Margaret began to communicate more freely and sought to provide wisdom and guidance on life and relationships. She encouraged Rhonda to seek in her male relationships men who could challenge her on an intellectual level. She understood the pitfalls of relationships between men and women who were not, minimally, intellectual peers. On reflection, Rhonda believes this was so strongly emphasized because Margaret's husband was not well-educated. As Rhonda dated, and as men entered and exited her life, Margaret always reiterated her basic premise that it was important for Rhonda to find a man who challenged her. She didn't want Rhonda to repeat her mistake.

Margaret also conveyed a strong message that many troubles in marital relationships were attributable to finances. It was her best advice that Rhonda seek a partner who was economically sound. She urged Rhonda to prepare herself to be financially independent and to always maintain credit in her own name. This was Margaret's way of protecting Rhonda should she find herself without her mate and in need of established credit. Margaret's experience was with a husband who always conducted business in cash and his lack of credit standing had caused difficulties for her family. Rhonda's own marriage has proven this guidance to be a truism. She has had to assume major financial responsibilities during periods when her husband has experienced long periods of unemployment.

Ironically, Margaret also eventually encouraged Rhonda to explore her sexuality. She told her that once she identified the right man, she should have sex with him. As they opened their communication, Rhonda learned that Margaret felt that she had been deprived of a sexually satisfying relationship during her marriage. She knew from her personal experience the importance of choosing a sexually compatible mate.

Margaret was married for fifty-three years and no one doubts that she loved her husband, even during the worst of times. It was not until she was in her sixties that she decided to leave him. Though they lived apart for eight years, they never divorced, and later reunited and lived with Rhonda and her family.

We bought a "humongous" old Victorian home. He and mom had come back together but were maintaining two separate apartments, and kind of honeymooning and sleeping over. He said this is really ridiculous, mine is too small and hers is too far. Rhonda, we are going to move in. Mom was pretty keen about it. Dad was there through the whole rehab process. Mom never stepped into the house until the day they moved in. That's how it started. They came in initially to live with us to share expenses so that we could get our feet on the ground. Then mom was diagnosed with cancer, so that was a definite; I was going to care for her. Then dad suddenly passed.

"JUST KEEP LIVING, WHEN YOU GET TO BE MY AGE, YOU'LL UNDERSTAND"

Rhonda has now been caring for Margaret for more than three years. As Margaret's mental state deteriorates from dementia, her care becomes more demanding and difficult. Rhonda receives good support from her sister and brothers, but she maintains the formidable responsibility for Margaret's primary care. This is an exacting situation for both women. Margaret, accustomed to being very sharp, is now frequently depressed and feels more inadequate as she looses her vitality, spirit and mental acuteness. Rhonda, on the other hand, longs for and regrets the loss of the Margaret she once knew, who challenged her and was there when she needed her.

There are times when I need mom to be the mom that used to be there. I could go and talk to her and she'd pray my prayer. My mother was a prayerful woman and I know that probably carried her through a lot of life challenges. That helps me as well. Sometimes I really miss that mother. We're close because I remember all the love and care that she gave to me. I feel like I owe it to her. I mean she was a terrific mom.

In some ways Rhonda is loosing a good friend, maybe even her best friend. She is compensating for this by developing strong bonds with other women and growing closer to her older sister. She sees the need for a strong female connection in her life and is gradually facing the fact that Margaret is no longer able to play that role. As Margaret's condition continues to deteriorate, Rhonda sees two primary reasons not to consider a nursing home. First, it is not the right thing to do, and second, she can't afford to do it. Either reason is sufficient to keep Rhonda motivated to maintain her personal strength and the faith to see her mother through this stage.

Margaret provided much wisdom for Rhonda to use in her life, and for this, Rhonda is eternally grateful. She credits Margaret with teaching her the value of work and the importance of prayer as a means to address those inevitable barriers women face. Most importantly she taught Rhonda that with love she could tolerate almost anything.

I'm becoming my mother. I can look in the mirror. I can see her actions. I can hear her words. All those things that she said to me, that once haunted me, I am my mother's child. Thank you, mom for showing me what a woman is; a beautiful, intelligent, loving, and supportive woman.

MARIE, MATTIE AND RENEE

The fears we create by our own thoughts are the cause of tremendous pressure, tension, pain and anguish. To live life with fulfillment, we must harness and define our thoughts and our thinking. Then we can live with faith, trust, self-awareness and love. Marie spent much of her life with her thoughts focused on finding any acceptable explanation of why her mother Renee would give her to Mattie to raise. Her thoughts are being harnessed and defined. She is realizing that the mother/daughter bond begins literally inside the mother's womb. Marie's life is more fulfilling as she experiences and understands the durability of the bond.

MARIE, MATTIE AND RENEE

It is after ten o'clock in the evening before Marie arrives for our conversation about her experiences as a daughter. We've talked on the telephone several times during the day attempting to find the best time to fit this conversation into her very busy schedule. When she arrives with her fiancé, they both look very weary, but Marie insists that she is up to the task. As she sends her fiancé to another room, she mentions that she spent the day moving to a new apartment. She is dressed in an oversized college tee-shirt, sandals and slightly baggy denim jeans with deep cuffs. Her black hair is almost shoulder length, naturally curly and in slight disarray framing her round light-skinned face. Though her appearance might reveal that she has been engaged in "manual labor," her natural beauty is definitive enough to overcome her somewhat lackadaisical attire. Marie has dark, expressive eyes and a warm and engaging smile. She is thirty-three years old and works in product management for a Fortune 100 technology company. The youngest child in a family of seven daughters and three sons, she was born and raised in a large, Midwestern city. Her mother, Mattie, began raising Marie at the age of four later formally adopting her when she was eleven years old. Mattie is seventy-four years old and is originally from the rural south. She is from a family of thirteen children, and although she has worked at numerous unskilled part-time jobs, she has spent most of her life as a homemaker raising her ten children. Renee, Marie's biological mother, is a fifty-year-old nurse living in the eastern part of the United States.

"GOD GIVES US OUR RELATIVES, BUT THANK GOD HE LETS US CHOOSE OUR FRIENDS"

The circumstances of Marie joining Mattie's family are somewhat complex. Renee, an Irish-American woman, had found herself pregnant after a brief affair with a Jamaican doctor. For reasons that are still unclear today, she decided not to keep her child. Prior to the birth of the child, she approached friends of a man she had begun to date. She asked them if they knew who might be interested in adopting her child. Relatives of Mattie's husband agreed to assist Renee by taking the child. Marie spent the first several years of her life with members of this family. When both of the women who were providing the primary care died before Marie's fourth birthday, there was no one else to raise her. Marie was then taken to live with Mattie, her husband and their nine children.

I knew that Mattie wasn't my mother, but I knew she had to become my mother because there was nobody else to take care of me. I knew this at four years old. I don't know how they explained it to me, but I always knew that. I didn't just wake up one day at four years old and this was my mother. I always knew she wasn't and then I remember at about eleven we did it legally. Any questions I had they finalized then. I had to talk to social workers. My parents had to talk to social workers. Then the entire big family went to court with me. We all went out to eat. It kind of jelled in my mind that I'm going to really be a part of them. That's how I felt about that episode.

Marie has many very positive memories about her childhood but when she summarizes her comments, they come directly to her mother, Mattie, whom she describes as a *wonderful woman*. Marie was the youngest child in Mattie's household and with the exception of one sister, eleven months older, the other five daughters were quite a bit older.

In many respects, the age difference among the daughters was an asset for Marie. The older girls would spend quality time and provide experiences that helped make childhood quite special. The older daughters were more like young aunts in the manner in which they took responsibility for helping Mattie with Marie. They would take her and the other younger sister on shopping trips, buy their clothes and take them on various outings for fun and amusement. Marie was involved in lots of activities as a child. Her dedicated older sisters made sure that she participated in organized programs such as tumbling and tap dancing. Everyone worked together to ensure that she had a well-rounded, happy and active childhood. Marie never lacked for anything.

Mattie was able to maintain the home and large family and perform the domestic functions that she understood and enjoyed. The older sisters would handle the rest. Mattie was a strict mother and although Marie doesn't remember more than two spankings, she intuitively knew Mattie's limits and rarely stepped outside of those clearly established parameters. Mattie had rules and Marie obeyed them.

I definitely was a compliant child and there were reasons I was compliant. But my personality was definitely more analytical and I was always questioning why. I wanted to be more defiant, but I was afraid to do anything that would upset my mother or make her think that I was a bad child or feel that she didn't want me there. You know those were the kinds of feelings that honestly entered my mind.

Mattie had been raised in the rural south and had dropped out of school at an early age to work on the family farm. This background led her to strongly promote the importance of Marie educating herself and preparing for a career. She didn't necessarily stress college, only the importance of acquiring skills and being positioned to find an enjoyable job. She wanted Marie to be independent and successful. Valuing the role of full-time mother, she also wanted Marie to know how to manage a household.

I thought she was kind of corny, like you've got to grow up and know how to type. You've got to know how to sew. You've got to know how to cook. You've got to know how to cook Sunday dinner. You can't just cook chicken and breakfast and all of that. You had to know how to cook greens or whatever. We all had to cook together and learn the way you fix soul food.

Marie is unequivocal about being a happy child and definitely believes that Mattie and her older sisters provided a solid, loving foundation. She had few worries and all around her were older siblings who supported her in every way. She was shown only the positive side of life and whenever anything negative happened, she would be sent to her room so as not to even hear things that might be troubling for a child.

You know, I really had a wonderful childhood because at twelve, I didn't even realize people got divorced. Even as some of my sisters started getting older and married, it was like that was what you were supposed to do. They only really showed us and taught us the positive things. We always had to go to the back room if something did happen in the family. I think with the things I didn't need to learn, my mother told me, "You'll always have time." So that was her message.

117

"IF IT AIN'T BROKE, DON'T FIX IT"

In the midst of this happy and seemingly healthy upbringing, Marie had only one issue that concerned her. That was the issue of her birth mother's decision to give her up for adoption. This was always a gnawing concern. Marie harbored guilt thinking about it because she was cared for and loved by Mattie and all of her family. Marie reasoned that talking about her adoption might somehow hurt Mattie. She never wanted to do anything to offend her or to make her feel that she was ungrateful. On the other hand, she could not help but speculate as to what would make Renee abandon her child. She could come up with no reasons that made any sense to her.

Why didn't she want to raise me? You know it was just like a daily thought of mine. How could a mother not want to raise her child? I always went through all the reasons. Was it money? We could have survived on whatever. At a certain age I found out that she was Caucasian and my father was Jamaican, so I said well maybe it was racial. And I said no, because when I went to high school there were so many children who would just tell you, " I'm biracial." So I didn't even see that there were any misgivings about that in society. I just could never come up with a reason. It just became my thing in life. Like children are sacred. I would prefer people just not have children if they're not going to take care of them. I didn't really understand that I needed to come to terms with all of this and that it really was a blessing. I wanted to tell her that we could've eaten grass and I don't care if we didn't have money. I just needed her. You know I wanted to tell her all these things. Why didn't she raise me and why would she go with a black man to Jamaica if she didn't want to raise the baby? I felt all these things as anger.

As Marie became a teenager, Mattie continued to be strict in her upbringing. Marie was a late bloomer and didn't start her menstrual or have any semblance of a date until her junior year in high school. She even attended her senior prom with a life long neighbor and family friend. When she left home to attend college, she began to become more independent. Her older sisters were, by this time, deeply involved in their families. Mattie did not want Marie to move away from home to attend college. She loved her and didn't want to relinquish the role she valued most, that of being a mother. She did not want to face the reality of having to deal with an empty nest for the first time in her adult life. Marie compromised and decided to attend a college in-state as opposed to her first choice which was in a state a substantial distance away. Throughout her college days, Marie had a tremendous network of support. Mattie provided the strong maternal figure and her older sisters covered the waterfront in their ability to address the range of issues that young women face.

I always had like a lot of support on those things. Having so many sisters it came to a point where I had like a different sister who I knew was strong, in different areas. I had one sister I knew I could talk to about boys and she would just be, that's her thing. Another sister, all she did was study. She loved school. She would rather be studying in the summer than going outside. So when you're trying to figure out what to major in or need some help with homework, I went to her. Another sister, whatever you needed to know about how you fix these clothes, put together the colors and sewing. You went to her.

Marie was basically doing fine as she entered her womanhood but she was still troubled by the circumstances of her birth and the mother, Renee, who gave her away.

Part of becoming a woman was me finding out more of who I was. I was always consumed with the mother thing. This mother thing was a central part of my life. The whole notion that mothers have to be treated special. Of course, I especially feel my mother should be treated special. She already had nine kids and took in another one. She has raised two others she didn't have to. So this is just out of love. I only became a woman when I felt forced. There's a part of me that just wanted to stay idealistic. You know, I can't get too far outside of this because I know there are bad things lurking. There's a whole reminder of not having my mother. It just always had an impact in my life.

"WHEN ONE DOOR CLOSES, ANOTHER ONE OPENS"

Marie successfully completed undergraduate school and later while working full-time began work on her master's degree in business administration. Marie was leading a busy life with school, work and an array of volunteer activities. She was maintaining a very close relationship with Mattie including making sure that she was home on Sunday's to help prepare Sunday dinner. She was developing a very special relationship with her favorite older sister who had two young daughters. When this sister was diagnosed with a terminal case of cancer, it was the thirty-one- year-old Marie whom she favored to take responsibility for the care of her twelve and sixteen-year-old daughters. The thought of this responsibility was awesome. Marie was now going to become a woman whether she liked it or not. Given Marie's strong appreciation for the importance of the mother/daughter relationship, when her sister died, there was no question that she would abide by her request.

Marie had given her word that she would be responsible for her nieces for the next two years. This meant a dramatic shift in her life. She gave up her independent, single lifestyle and moved with her nieces to an apartment upstairs from Mattie. She nurtured her younger pubescent niece through the pain of the lost of a mother when she was just graduating from elementary school. She also provided love, counsel and advice to the niece who was soon to be entering college and womanhood. Mattie helped Marie by doing what she did best, taking care of the basic needs and making sure that there was always a big soulful Sunday dinner. Marie was managing to maintain her life as a professional woman, a student, and as a parent while continuing to volunteer and have a semblance of a personal life. It was a tough time for her overall, and certainly not a time to be confronted with her *mother thing*. At twenty-eight years old, it was hard for Marie to understand why Renee would need to come into her life for the very first time.

"Do Not Think That Your Poor Judgment Is Cause For Emergency Action On My Part"

I answer my phone and there's a doctor on the line who says he's Renee's doctor in another state and that she was pretty ill. Mostly mentally ill. He was her psychologist. She's really suffering a lot because of giving up her daughter. I didn't know that was even her name. I just said, I hope this is not a cruel joke someone is playing on me. He said no, that it was real, that she wanted to talk to me but she wanted to know if he could intervene for her. This went on for several months of conversations with just him. By him being a psychologist, I could honestly say that was a blessing. He was able to wean the situation on me. I think I would have been more completely overwhelmed if she had just called me out of the blue. She ended up doing that because I could never agree to meet her. I just said that this was far too much for me to handle. I had just reconciled in my own head how it's so easy to say well no one will help me with any little thing. Just any little thing that would happen and if I could attribute it to the fact I'm adopted, that's what I would do. Everything wrong was because you didn't have your real mother. It was just really not making me a positive person.

Initially, Marie told only her best girlfriend about the developing situation with Renee. She could not imagine herself going to Mattie. She felt it would be an insult to Mattie to even mention something called a "biological mother"

120

after twenty-eight years and no contact. Marie had always tried to make herself feel as though Mattie was her real mother because she had certainly treated her that way. Further, as always, Marie was the last one who would want to do anything that would be upsetting to Mattie. Deep inside, Marie just wanted the whole situation to just take care of itself and go away. Marie was very uncomfortable as the calls kept coming from the psychologist but she was never really curious. She had made up in her mind long ago that there was no acceptable explanation or reason that Renee should have given her away. She continued to keep these developments away from Mattie and she continued to refuse to meet Renee.

So I don't know, I felt like I had no reason to do this. Although being very honest, I felt originally as though she was physically sick. Here she was dying and she wanted me to reconcile with her for her purposes. I didn't think I could give her that. My comments to the doctor were it's between her and God. I just didn't want to be a part of it. He was very adamant and very understanding, doing what doctors do well. Then he started to act as if I was one of the patients.

Eventually after more than a year of stress and overwork, Marie was literally becoming ill. She was being a parent, a successful businesswoman, an involved member of her community. She was pressing herself terribly hard. At the same time she was holding inside this highly sensitive situation with Renee. In an almost hysterical and emotional conversation, Marie finally told Mattie that she had heard from Renee. Mattie was by no means insulted or hurt. She helped Marie to see the need to meet Renee and to determine if there might be a potential relationship between them. She refused to accept any of Marie's "mother bashing" and told her it was important that she deal with her circumstances. She listened carefully to Marie and was calm, wise and as patient as always. As she often did throughout Marie's life, she used one of her favorite phrases, " Everything will work out, everything will be alright."

You could tell my mom the worst thing in the world. It wasn't that big of a deal for her. She was always so calm and patient just like well, everything will work out. And she'd tell us that about everything. Everything would be alright. She would just sit there and listen to you. She'd just be like, " It will all work out." Now I see some things I've learned following her reaction. You can't get all riled up about everything and you just have to trust and know that everything will be alright. It might not be the way you define alright. That's another thing she taught me. It's going to be alright just because it's going to be all right.

"WHAT GOES AROUND COMES AROUND"

Things are alright for Marie these days. She has done a lot of growing up in only a few years. She has met Renee and through their developing relationship, she has learned and grown. Renee's manic depressive condition is improving. She still has to clear up aspects of her life including her relationship with Marie. Marie has learned a lot about Renee. Renee has lived her life as though she were a light-skinned African-American woman. She has lived exclusively in African-American communities, always dated only African-American men, and eventually married and had two sons with an African-American man. Renee has kept secrets from everyone. Her husband never knew about Marie. She never told her obviously biracial sons that she was a Caucasian and they have grown up with serious personal and psychological issues related to their racial identity. Like Marie, they hold bitterness and resentment toward Renee. Renee recently told her very dark-skinned eighteen-year-old daughter that she was adopted. She too, is contending with an identity struggle centered around her skin color and other issues, and a recently located biological mother who has totally rejected her.

Marie is putting the pieces of her life together and is learning more about herself. She is learning not to focus on what she didn't have in life because her biological mother didn't raise her. She is trying to focus on all the wonderful gifts she has received in life, especially Mattie. She is ever so grateful to Mattie whom she will always view as her mother. She feels a tremendous sense of freedom now that everything is out in the open.

Marie is beginning to fully understand her spiritual dimension and believes that her faith in God has been the critical factor to carry her through the difficult times. She is establishing a solid relationship with her new brothers and has a special interest in her new adopted sister. She empathizes with the pain she is going through as an adopted child who feels rejected by her birth mother. Marie has met a man that she loves and plans to marry soon. She is continuing a role as a surrogate parent to her nieces and is delighted with the beautiful young women they have become with her help and guidance. Finally, Marie is testing the waters with Renee.

I guess I could never call her my mother. I still don't really respect her a lot. I guess the most prevailing thought about her before I met her is you can get through anything. I just had a checklist of things in my mind of why she couldn't raise her child and to me none of those jived out. She did try to tell me why several times. She does not really talk about my father. She doesn't know anything about him too much other than his name. They conceived me in Jamaica and that was the last time she saw him. He doesn't even know I exist. I really don't know why she gave me up. I told her I didn't want to know and nothing is going to make me understand. But she had to get if off of her chest so it was some kind of healing for her. She became manic depressive and you know just all these secrets. There's a secret about each child.

I wanted to kind of prove to her, and I've told her this, that I'm a good person. I was going to be able to do all these things so that she would be proud of me. I think that's another thing. Initially, especially when I was in graduate school, when she first called me, it was like she had found a diamond. She found any and every opportunity to contact me. I mean she would call me at 3:00 in the morning 7:00 in the morning. There was just no respect for my schedule. It's like, I got you now. Even after that she sent me a lot of e-mails, cards, fresh flowers, just any and everything. I had to finally ask her if I could be the one in control. It was just a little bit too much. It was just starting to cause me stress. So now she really doesn't initiate a lot.

In a sense I understand myself more. Just physically, I look like her, my health conditions, personality, which really shocks me. If I wasn't even around her, I'm not sure how we have so many similarities, likes and dislikes, foods, books, and writing. Yeah, she likes the things I like. We have a lot more interests in common. Genes are very powerful.

PEARL AND FANNIE

We are all some mother's daughter, and the role our mothers' play in
our lives cannot be understated. The truth is, being a mother may be the
most difficult and the most important job a woman can have in life.
Pearl loved her mother Fannie dearly but knew early in life that she never
wanted to be like Fannie. Pearl decided to control her life and reserve
her real love only for her children. Pearl learned that children are blessings and being a mother is her career and her life.

PEARL AND FANNIE

Pearl warmly greets me on the afternoon of my arrival to her small high rise
apartment in a large northern city. She is seventy-three-years old, with a complexion light enough that one might assume her to be biracial. She covers her
naturally curly, shiny, silver hair with a dark brown wig. Standing only a couple of inches over five feet tall and somewhat above her desired weight, she is
dressed in a colorful caftan and a matching turban. Hanging on the wall near
the entrance to this modest apartment is a very large photograph of Pearl as
young woman. Immediately one is struck by her outstanding beauty and
knockout figure. Nearby, neatly arranged in a glass enclosed cabinet, are
crowded shelves displaying framed color photographs of all of her children
and grandchildren.

Pearl, a divorcee, was married for almost thirty years and is originally from
rural Alabama. She is the mother of seven children. Five are daughters. Pearl
spent most of her life as a stay-at-home housewife and mother, working only
occasionally for the postal service during the Christmas holiday rush. She is
the seventh child and only living daughter, of thirteen children born to Fannie,
also from rural Alabama. Like Pearl, Fannie was a full-time mother and
housewife who did domestic work for white families in her southern community.

Pearl had the typical lifestyle of one growing up in the rural south in the late
1920s. She remembers her family raising chickens and hogs, cooking on a
wood-burning stove and swimming in creeks. Fannie, as a mother to such a
large clan, was totally domestic. She could cook, sew and handle almost any
medical emergency using her homespun techniques. The shy, quiet spoken
Fannie, was totally involved in the care of her children and her husband.

Pearl recalls Fannie as being unassertive, compliant and humble when it came to interfacing with her husband, a very handsome man with a gregarious personality and a quick wit. He made all of the decisions for the household. Fannie's role was to execute them. The couple would argue occasionally primarily because of his periodic philandering and flirtatious behavior with women. Pearl doesn't remember them ever fighting because this simply was not Fannie's style. She would try to make her point and then, eventually, she would capitulate to the needs and desires of her husband. Even as a child, Pearl privately questioned why Fannie did not stand up for herself and why she accepted such a secondary role in the management of her household, not to mention why she tolerated her husband's indiscretions.

Pearl and Fannie were very close, as were the all of the four daughters to each other and to Fannie. Pearl loved being around Fannie. Many times while the other siblings were engaged in outdoor activities and enjoying the frivolity of childhood, Pearl would be in the kitchen assisting Fannie. She would help her prepare meals, wash dishes or do whatever she could to be helpful. Although Fannie never requested this assistance, Pearl made it her practice to voluntarily help Fannie before she would join the other children in play.

Pearl was raised to value education and was considered smart in school. With the exception of making sure her children attended church, there was probably nothing more important to Fannie than assuring that her children behaved and did well in school. Pearl recalls that Fannie would help her with her homework and read to her. She would ignore her schemes claiming illness when she wanted to avoid going to school. Being somewhat of a mischievous child, with classical " middle child" characteristics, Pearl was known to create cleverly contrived plots to avoid attending school. Notwithstanding this tendency, she was smart enough to be moved ahead in grade and was younger than most of her peers when she began high school.

When I didn't get my homework out, I knew I would get a whipping in class. So I would want to stay away from school. I'd pretend that I was sick. She'd send me anyway and when I got to school I would prolong it so that I could come back home. I remember one time getting a piece of sand paper and smearing it all over my arms and going back home telling her the teacher whipped me and blistered my arm up. She went over there and balled the teacher out. When she found out that I had lied, then she whipped me right there in the class in front of all the kids.

Pearl entered puberty in a world without Kotex or Tampons and was not openly informed about what was happening to her body. Fannie was far too shy to discuss such matters. Though quite outspoken and opinionated on most subjects, Pearl learned from Fannie that these were very private subjects that were not appropriate for discussion. What she did learn about her development as a woman came primarily from an older sister. Pearl's basic attitude was that sex was an obligatory act performed by women for the satisfaction of men. The only good thing about it as far as women were concerned was that it had the potential to result in the giving of life. Today Pearl continues to view these matters as off-limits for discussion.

Unlike most of her female peers, Pearl went on to complete the eleventh grade without getting pregnant or married. She dropped out of school prior to graduation in order to work full-time and with a plan to eventually return to school to complete her high school requirements.

"Money Can't Buy Love"

Pearl developed into a beautiful young woman who, although much sought after by men, never viewed herself quite that way. She did enjoy fashionable clothes, jewelry and wearing makeup, but was never "stuck on" herself. For many years, beginning while she was still in high school, it was clear to her and her family that she was the favorite of an older man from a prominent family in the area. Pearl was not especially fond of this man even though he showered her with attention and gifts. But she was impressed with him, both due to his age and the lifestyle afforded by his social status. His family owned several small businesses and they were leaders in one of the local churches. Fannie saw in this man and his middle class family, an opportunity for Pearl to "marry up." After aggressive courting, that's exactly what Pearl decided to do. She never did return to school and she never really forgave Fannie for the pressure she had felt to marry a man that she really did not love.

Well I didn't really choose him. My mother chose him for me. She just really wanted me to marry him because she figured that he was older than me and he could teach me the things that I didn't know. In other words, he came from a very nice family. They were very classy and they were religious. And back in that time they were considered as wealthy. She would tell me all the time why don't I marry him. She knew he liked me. So when I married him, she was very happy.

Pearl's early married life was exciting. Her husband had joined the Navy and this provided an opportunity for travel and excitement. She spent the first several years of her marriage moving around the country and indeed the world. She was exposed to a world she did not know existed and her experiences took

.er far beyond the small "country" town of her childhood. Although she was frequently located long distances away from her Alabama roots, she maintained a close and loving relationship with Fannie. She would return home often while her husband was aboard ship serving on various assignments and during periods of military conflict. She would leave her young son with Fannie while she rendezvoused in various locations with her husband. She also returned home for an extended stay when she was ready to deliver her second child who was her first daughter. Eventually, her husband left military service and Pearl, now with two young children, located her family to a large city in the north. It was now time to settle down. The excitement was over. She had to learn to live on a day- to-day basis with a man that she didn't really know that well, not to mention love.

"You Made Your Bed, So Lay In It"

On one dimension, Pearl was very much like Fannie in that she eventually had a large family and totally enjoyed her children. Like Fannie she took great pleasure in being a mother and was completely dedicated to family. She loved her role as mother and had no aspirations other than to be the best possible mother that she could be. She was able to find complete fulfillment in giving birth, raising and loving her children.

My children were my happiness. That's why I stayed married as long as I could. I just wanted to be around my children and wanted my children to be happy. So as long as they were happy, I was happy, even just being around them. I used to always say that I don't crave luxuries, like diamonds and minks and stuff like that. I like ordinary stuff. I like nice things. But as long as I had and could be with my children, and had a roof over my head, food, shelter and could clothe them, I was happy. In other words, my happiness was dependent on my children. The interesting thing about it is that I never wanted a lot of children. I just said I would like to have one child to prove myself a woman. But after I kept getting pregnant and feeling the life inside me, well, I wanted all of them. When I felt them moving around in me, I started feeling love. I didn't want anything to happen to it. I've never regretted that I had all those children. I was proud of all of them.

Unlike Fannie, however, Pearl controlled her household and her relationship with her husband. Even though she did not work, she controlled the finances and took leadership in the families decision making. She was a no nonsense woman and expected, even demanded, that things be handled her way. Her husband's paychecks were turned over to her and he'd be given an allowance to handle his needs. Pearl also demanded respect as a woman. She considered herself as "the prize" and expected to be treated special. She did not intend to tolerate the position that Fannie had accepted in her marriage. Pearl's husband, being older and married to such a beautiful woman, accepted this positioning in the early years of the marriage. This would however change dramatically later as alcohol became the control in his life.

Pearl and her husband began a pattern of endless fighting and arguing. There was little show of love and affection. Pearl was always struggling to take care of her children through the storms caused by her husband's alcoholism and gambling. There were car accidents, jail time and all manner of family disruption. Often he'd come home late from work and drunk and Pearl would be on the warpath. Unlike the way Fannie handled such situations, Pearl was forceful and aggressive in her approach to her husband. They'd actually physically fight, until her children reached the age that this behavior became troubling to them.

The primary issues that caused difficulty between Pearl and her husband were his drinking and money. These issues often were tied together to create the conflicts. On payday, Pearl would often pace nervously, watch the clock and telephone his favorite watering holes to see why he had not come home with money for his family. The later he was, the more her tension. There were occasions when he'd arrive having spent lots of money gambling along the way. This would create real disturbances as Pearl regrouped to figure out how she would make ends meet. Somehow, she always managed to provide an environment where her children rarely lacked for anything that they needed.

Pearl had learned a valuable lesson from Fannie's position of almost complete deference and dependency. Although she was a full-time mother and housewife with no income, she learned that it was important to have some money of her own. Pearl would scrimp and cut corners in order to be able to put aside a few dollars that she could use for her special needs and those of her children.

My mother had a good marriage. But she didn't really teach me anything about that because I had a mind of my own. She was real humble. She thought she had to obey my father. He was the boss over her. And I couldn't see no man just bossing me. I wanted to go like fifty/fifty or either me being more of the boss than he was. It was just in my mind. I didn't need nobody who would try to control me. It was just understood that he would have to bring the money to me. It wasn't no big deal to him because, you know, he never refused it or anything until at the end.

It was no secret to anyone close to Pearl that she stayed married because of her children. She states almost adamantly that love had nothing to do with the longevity of her marriage. Her marriage lasted almost thirty years and it was only after Pearl realized that she could no longer totally sacrifice her own happiness for that of her children that she decided to leave. She also felt that the fifty/fifty balance she desired was tipping in the direction of her husband. By this time Pearl's four oldest children were in college or were living independently. She left her husband taking her three youngest daughters to begin a life as a single parent.

When he started getting tight with giving me the money, then I was making plans on leaving. I just couldn't control him like I wanted to. He was just so overbearing because of alcohol and everything. I just had to have a life of my own. I took it as long as I could. So when I'd seen that he wasn't going to get any better, after my younger kids all were in elementary school, I just couldn't take it anymore. I just had to leave. I never regretted it. I think that's the best move I ever made. I was happier and content.

"BLOOD IS THICKER THAN WATER"

Pearl was determined that being a single parent would not cause her three young daughters any disadvantages. Having successfully raised four children in a two parent environment, she never wanted to feel that leaving her husband and seeking her own happiness had any negative impact on the remaining daughters. She did everything for them and was completely a hands-on mother.

Pearl also began to date and entered into a relationship that was to last more than twenty years. In this new relationship, Pearl was again able to exercise her favored position of having the upper hand. It was only when she felt one single instance of disrespect that the relationship ended. Pearl telephoned his home one afternoon and a woman answered the phone. That was it. No questions asked, no explanations required. Pearl ended the relationship on the spot, never spoke to him again and never looked back. She has not had a serious relationship since that time and has completely devoted her life to being a mother and grandmother.

Today, Pearl lives alone and is quite content and happy. Though she is still attractive and gets the attention of spry senior men, she has absolutely no interest in any type of relationship outside of her family. She maintains strong and loving relationships with all of her children and grandchildren and lets everyone know that her children are the most important people in her life. For her, nothing has higher priority than her role as mother. She can recite with much pride the date, day of week, time of day and birth weight of each of her seven children. She proudly states that, *my career was mostly raising children while enjoying it.* She remembers and acknowledges the birthdays of her dozen grandchildren and has personally nurtured all of them. Her children attest that she has been there for them whenever and wherever she has been needed. She is an absolute matriarch and her "kingdom" has lovingly dubbed her "Queen Pearl."

Pearl has passed on to her five daughters some of the messages that she received from Fannie and many that she created for herself. Each of her daughters values their independence and their ability to take care of themselves and their families. Each has a strong self-concept and though not quite as strong willed as Pearl, have reasonably managed their lives and personal relationships. She has lots of advice for her daughters as well as for other women. Some of it she took from Fannie, but much of it is her own wisdom learned from living life.

I had an idea of my own about raising my children. I didn't raise my daughters like she did. I just wanted my daughters to be more outgoing than she was. I'd tell them to never let a man get them under control. To be their own boss and satisfy themselves. I think a woman should please herself as much as she pleases the man. Don't never let a man take control of you. Stand on your own two feet. You don't need no man who you have to ask for stuff because a man knows that a woman has needs. He shouldn't have to wait for you to ask him. He should just volunteer to do for you.

Be as nice to him as he is to you. Just don't be so weak for him. Make him have responsibilities for you. I don't believe in being weak for a man. I believe in a man doing everything for the woman. I only like the men who are nice to my daughters. As long as they are nice to my daughters, I like them. But when they start to getting mean and out of the ordinary then, I am that way with them.

I always would try to tell them to keep a little change on hand just in case of an emergency. And another thing I would always say was to do their cleaning at night because I figured you don't ever know what might happen overnight. I would tell them to have friends, but never trust women so much as to tell them all of your personal business. I don't think nobody should know everything about your business. And most of all, I would just tell them to pray. That's the best answer.

DAUGHTERS SHARE MOTHER'S WISDOM

SHORT RECOLLECTIONS

SCHENA AND LEE ESTHER

Try as I might, my adolescent psyche could never comprehend why mama, intelligent and intuitive as she was, repeatedly asked questions with such obvious, sole answers. She did so expecting a response no matter how many times she inquired, and it was not unusual for mama's askings to number heavenward on any given day. In particular, mama constantly wanted to know "Is Fat Meat Greasy?" The only response to that question was singular and affirmative or the only response mama would hear anyway and that answer was always, "yes, ma'am, yes, ma'am; yes, ma'am." Mama got no argument from me. As I saw it, fat meat is greasy whether it is ribs on a grill, whether it is flavoring in some greens, or whether it is her chicken (me) with one-fourth jar of Vaseline slapped on my four cheeks. My youthful mind wanted to know why ask a question, if you know the answer? When I answered as rehearsed, without fail, apparently all mama wanted to do was challenge me with either, "I don't think you believe fat meat is greasy," or a "You don't act like fat meat is greasy." And talk about slowing a roll—ah, that is interrupting one's plans: When mama delivered her query with a quiet boom, the gravity of her vocal chords had a knack of wrapping themselves around my legs stopping me. Dead In My Tracks. Like when I was ten and mama said I was smelling myself. Or when I was sixteen and she said I was thinking I was grown. If my adolescent psyche failed to comprehend the value to this homogenous line of interrogation, my young-adult mind was the first to appreciate the advantages the deliberation of this question was to inspire. Salvation not being the least of these advantages, I commenced to asking my-SELF is fat meat greasy, as if to subvert my own hardheaded tendencies. Most likely, what mama intended herself. And now that I have a chicken of my own, if I am astonished by the persistence with which this query shows up in my speech as my three-year-old navigates his way through life, I remain undeterred by the perplexity of his stare.

ANDREA AND CAROLYN

Andrea, you never finish a job completely. You half do everything. You ought to care a little bit more about what you do. You're gonna mess up everything if you half do some things.

SERENA AND PEARL

I had been riding a boy's bike and had hurt myself. I had carefully placed the bloody panties in the laundry basket, thinking if I buried them, my mother would not see them. When she did her laundry, of course, she finds a pair of bloody underpants. That very weekend she sent both my sister and me to my aunt's house where we were told the facts of life. I recall how my mother stored the sanitary napkins in the linen closet. She monitored the supply, and knew when my cycle would begin and end. She would even insist that I show her the used pad. I hated this, and found it quite embarrassing. She said that she wanted to make sure that everything was coming out properly and that the color and flow was normal. Although, this may have been partly true, this periodic check was a surefire way of her knowing that the cycle had actually occurred.

ANONYMOUS

My mother, she didn't communicate. She just worked. I mean, she's a hard worker. That's all I ever saw my mother do was work. She would work at night and we all had school during the day. When she came home, she was tired. She had ten kids and I was the only daughter. That was it. I don't remember her doing anything but work.

ANONYMOUS

I did not have a good relationship with my mother growing up. When I was twenty-two, I remember something inappropriate that my grandmother did. My mother, who never said bad things about anyone, got so mad at my grandmother that she started talking about her childhood. I heard all these things about her childhood and her relationship with my grandmother. I didn't know how upsetting that relationship was and how it had impacted on the things she did at the time. When I heard this, I said, "oh my goodness, no wonder this happened or that happened to me." Now we are very close. It totally changed our relationship. We need not only an understanding of our mothers as people but also an understanding about how they grew up.

HELEN AND PEARL

My mother ran a strict household. It was very orderly. Everything had a place. As it related to education or discipline, or whatever, you were expected to do certain things. When you did not do those things, there were consequences. So typically speaking, growing up, I did what I needed to do to avoid the consequences. She had issues around having certain life standards and

133

about whom I could have a relationship with whether it was a male or female. She'd say, "You can't play with them because they're not clean and well groomed and you cannot play with them because they curse. You cannot play with them if they don't like your siblings." There was no such thing as my having a friend that disliked any of my other family members. As it related to the opposite sex, it was the same thing. The guy had to be courteous. He had to present a certain image. I think those attitudes were very strong and perhaps at times, I did not understand them. But I think, as I grew older, I clearly understood what she meant. And probably, in terms of being strict, those things ultimately served to protect me.

DIANE AND LULA

My mother was fond of saying, "Nothing beats a failure but a try." I often recalled those words as I strived to obtain a college education. I believe those words were instrumental in helping me to achieve an A.A. in Liberal Arts, a B.S. in Special Education, and an M.S. in Education. My mother passed away on July 22, 1985. I still remember many of the things that she taught me, but what really makes me struggle to keep going when I'm tired, or when I really want to quit, are those words, "nothing beats a failure but a try."

JOYCE AND ELOISE

We lived with my grandmother for a while when my mother divorced, and my grandmother became a surrogate mother while my mother worked. My mother bought her own house and moved out when my grandmother started telling my brother that he did not have to do housework and that was what the girls had to do.

BETTYE AND RUBY

My mother always said to me as a child, "Stay and act like a child." I never understood the meaning behind those words. Now I do. As a child, I didn't have anything to really worry about. My mom took care of my needs. As an adult, life is not a bed of roses. Don't rush growing up. Be that child as long as God lets you.

WENDY AND JOHNNIE MAE

My mother always used to tell me when I was growing up that she loved me and liked me. Being my mother, she had to love me but she also liked me as a person. That still means the world to me. She still loves me and likes me. I love her and also like her very much.

SERENA AND PEARL

My mother's daughters are all shapes, sizes, and hues. Growing up though, the different complexions of her daughters raised the most attention and conversation from others outside the family. As one of the darker-hued daughters of a light-skinned woman, she taught me to value myself as her "pretty brown child" when others would draw the comparison between me and my mother, and me and my lighter skinned sister. I remember as a child, adding some bleach to my bath water thinking that it would lighten my skin. She was appalled and quickly removed me from the tub. I really didn't understand what I had done wrong. Initially, I thought that she was upset because bleach was not something to be wasted in the bath water. She took me aside and, as her anger subsided, proceeded to take considerable time to talk with me. She told me how beautiful I was and how I needed to be proud of my deep brown skin. I never forgot that incident.

TANIESHA AND LOUISE

My mother would always say, "When you want something, no matter how big or small or how much it costs, just ask for it." I know this taught me a valuable lesson about taking things that did not belong to me and stealing.

LINDA AND LULA

My mother always talked about "being hardheaded" and she'd say, "A hard-head makes a soft butt." When I was a kid, it meant when I tell you to do A and not B because B is bad and you do B anyway, I'm going to soften your butt by beating it. Now it means to me that if I'd rather listen to the advice of the inexperienced person than that given by the experienced person, then I will end up suffering in some way or another.

WANDA

There are no words of wisdom that I can remember from my mother. She never talked to me as a child or passed down any little golden nuggets to cherish my life through. So from that experience of growing up with silent parents (unless you were getting a beating for getting into something), I pass the following on to my children:

Children, silence is not golden, because where there is silence, there is a lack of communication. When you don't talk, you can't find out who your children really are. They must be allowed to express themselves, to talk about how they feel, or what happened in school. They need to be heard. Parents need to take the time to listen. The days of being seen and not heard are over. Our children must be heard so that we as mothers can learn who our children are, and direct what they will become. Our children are our future and we must learn to listen to our leaders of tomorrow.

HELEN AND PEARL

My mother enjoyed having children around her. I cannot stand children. I have one and I love him dearly, but that's enough. I think deep down inside what it really was, was my having the clarity, early on, around what it takes to raise children. I saw what you have to give of yourself and watched my mother give and sacrifice. I made a decision that that's not what I wanted to do. I oftentimes wondered did the children keep my mother from really being the person that she wanted to be? She would never say that, and I am not so sure she ever even felt that way. I never saw my mother talking about, "Oh, all these kids and no money." It was always like, "We don't have any money and this is the best there is, so let's get going here. You don't have new shoes, shine those old ones up and put the ribbons in your hair and you'll look great." I could never be the person that she was. It would have killed me. I don't know what that means. I acknowledge who I am and I'm basically pretty selfish, pretty self-centered. I could never give of myself the way that my mother gave of herself. Isn't that awful?

BRENDA AND JESSIE

I love my mother so much I can't even imagine her not being here. I mirror myself after her and try to do everything for my kids that she did for me. She'd do all the little things. Like in the mornings readying you for school, you may lose your earring. By the time I got home, momma had found it. Maybe one morning, on a gym day, your gym shoe was lost. By the time I got home, momma had found it. Anything we lost, she had found it by the time we got home.

DE-DEE AND CEAL JANE

From the time I was very young, I remember my mother, a woman with an eighth grade education, always saying to me, "Girl, get yo education, so you don't have to be no floor mat for some man." At the time, I did not quite understand what she meant. But as I grew older, it became clearer. She was telling me to get an education so that I would not have to depend on a man to take care of me. That lesson has served me well. Because I did get my education, I have always looked at a man for who he was and not for what he could do for me financially. That has been freeing and liberating. You see, my mother believed in education for women before it was popular and she passed that belief on to me.

DAISY AND JESSIE

When I had my first child I remember she said, "Don't call me when you go into labor because I'll be just too worried and upset. My blood pressure would get too high if you call me. Just call me after you have it." So I took her at her word and I picked up the phone and I said momma I just had a little girl. And she said, "Oh my God Lord Have Mercy you're making my blood pressure go up. You've got to be kidding, why didn't you call me."

EARLINE

My mother never really communicated with me. I had to more or less, learn from other women, watching and listening. I never had too much to say, I just watched. I would say to myself, I'm not taking that. There were a lot of things going on in my life at home that I didn't feel my mother stepped forward to protect me from. I just said, I'm not going to let anybody sexually abuse me. I don't care who they are, and if my mother won't stand up for me, then I'm out. I left at seventeen.

CHERYL

I didn't grow up with my mother. I grew up with my grandmother. She used to tell me, "If you are having sex, come and tell me." At that time, I wasn't having sex and I just thought that when the time came I would let her know. The time came, but I didn't let her know. I became pregnant and when I was five months, my sister told her. At that moment, I saw tears in my grandmother's eyes. From then on, my relationship with my grandmother has been total chaos. She never really told me but I always knew it was because she expected so much out of me.

ROSA AND ANNIE

My mother never talked to me about sex. I would have to talk to my grandmother. She was old to me and she never talked about the pill or anything. A lot could have been prevented if she had. I got pregnant at thirteen and I got pregnant at fifteen. I had my first true boy friend at thirteen and he is still my husband at thirty-two. It's very romantic to most people. He's four years older than I am. I tell my daughters to get their education to make sure they are prepared and able to go it alone. I don't want them to be with one man all of their lives. I have urges to know what other men are like, how they treat you as opposed to this one man. I want them to know that before they make a decision so they won't feel like they should have made another one. That's what I want them to get out of all of this. Don't settle.

DAISY AND JESSIE

She had a strong opinion an "if you lay down with dogs you come up with fleas" kind of an attitude. For instance when I was a teenager, if I had a friend who was pregnant or known to be sexually active, her comment was, "You don't have anything in common with her. Why would you want to hang with her?" Her attitude was that once you started being sexually active, you were an official woman. I remember she used to always say you only have eighteen years to be a little girl and the rest of your life to be a woman. She encouraged us to try to maintain that innocence of being a little girl.

ANONYMOUS

My mother didn't talk about any of that stuff. She didn't open her mouth about anything. My mother would take us to our grandmother. Grandmother would sit us down on this couch and she would start talking to us about the birds and the bees and giving us some symbolism. My mother would be gone because she couldn't handle it. Anything that dealt with pain and things like that, mother would take us to grandmother. She didn't want to deal with those unpleasantries.

CAREY

I am eighty-four years old and I never had children, but I've had a wonderful life. That's the only way I can express it. I don't know if I would have been a particularly good mother. That has never been one of my burning desires, never something I felt I needed. I have Godchildren and I lavish love and things upon them, but then they go home. I like it that way.

JACQUELINE AND JESSIE

I think the biggest and the strongest message that my mother sent to me was on relationships. My mother was a strong woman when it came to a man. She would not grieve over a man or just be bothered. She was intolerant of nonsense when it came to men. I think I tried to emulate that to impress her. I remember my first boyfriend, my high school sweetheart. I remember having an argument with him on the phone because he was taking someone else to the prom, and my mother overheard it. She immediately made me get off of the phone and told me not to talk to him any more and to forget him. She said that there were plenty of other men out there and he ought to be proud to be with me. She meant everything she said. She was building my self-esteem and my character as far as values, and what I would stand for and what I would not stand for. My mother would always say, "Don't chase a man, let him chase you." So I don't chase men, they have to chase me. She got across the message that I am the prize, that I know my worth.

I realized when I went away to college and my mother wasn't around, I got somewhat weak. I always said if my mother knew this, she would be so disappointed. I needed her in college. Because she was not around, there were certain things that I settled for. I knew that if I still lived under her roof, I just wouldn't have. I would have tried to impress her. So a lot of that stuck with me because I think in relationships today, I'm very strong. Some people ask me where do I get this characteristic or this trait from, and I say, from my mother.

DORIS AND MYRA

My first marriage was my first love, and it was a way of getting away from home. When I divorced my first husband, I felt that I had done something wrong because I always thought about my mother. I'd think, my mother stayed married, why can't I. My mother had eight children and she wasn't about to walk away. She was married for sixty years. Then I thought, this is another day and time. I was stagnant. I didn't want to stay. I needed to move on and to move ahead. My mother felt that if you are being mistreated, don't stay. She felt that you should try to do your best to keep it together, but if it's a matter of being mistreated, don't stay with him. I stayed with him, I'm sure, longer than I needed to have stayed. After a point, I decided my mother's life is not my life. I tell my daughter to do whatever you need to do to make yourself happy without hurting other people. Take care of yourself, because nobody else will. That's sort of the way I feel now.

ELINOR AND GINA

My mother always told me when I would go out and party, "If you meet a man in the club, leave him there." I live by this rule today. I know for a fact that my future husband will not be a bar rat!

SERENA AND PEARL

I remember the evening before my marriage. I was just twenty years old and had completed my second year in college. As my mother busily worked in the kitchen staring in the pot and never looking up, she asked me had I had sex with my husband- to-be. Though I had, and thus broken her rule of no premarital sex, given her strict upbringing, I responded an adamant NO. She looked up directly at me and said, "Girl that's like buying a pair of shoes and not knowing what size they are."

JOYCE AND BERTHA

When I was about eight-years-old, I remember my mother calling my seven sisters and me into the bedroom. She grouped all of us around the bed and made us get on our knees to pray. She led us in a prayer asking for husbands for each of us. She described the kind of men she wanted us to have and made us repeat after her. She had spent her whole life going with a married man and wanted something different for her daughters. She felt that if we started to pray for a husband early in life, then maybe by the time we were grown, we could have a man of our own, and not one that belonged to another woman. So we kneeled down beside that bed and prayed for husbands, all eight of us.

BRENDA AND JESSIE

I had always had just one boyfriend and had never ever been into mischief or anything like that. She told me, "You're too young and too pretty to be just having one man." I'm thinking, now my momma wants me to be a whore. Now that I'm older, I realize it wasn't that. What she was saying was that I was too young to be tied up with just one person. I understand everything behind those words today.

DEBORAH

One of the things my mother taught me is that you never give up on a man, no matter what. My father did all kinds of things, even some sexual things to my sister who was not his child. My mother knew this and she just stayed and stayed and stayed. She was the type of person who felt that as long as the man is taking care of the home as far as finances, then everything is okay. I think this attitude set me back. I was going through a domestic relationship where there was fighting all the time. When the physical abuse stopped, there was mental abuse. Finally, through a Public Aid program, I started meeting and working around positive women that were strong. I started to speak up and not say what he wanted to hear just because he was the breadwinner. I said, I could either break the cycle or deal with it. For three years, I just went on and dealt with it, just kept dealing with it. This year I decided that I wasn't going to go through another year unhappy and miserable. When I actually threw him out, my mother called and said, " We don't give up, you don't do that." It's so hard for me. When I find myself needing something, I will call him. I feel that my mother really messed me up with that, because if I didn't feel that I had to depend on him, I wouldn't keep him around. It's unfair to me. It's unfair to him.

BRENDA AND JESSIE

We knew she had a boyfriend and he was real good to us and good for her. There were three young girls still at home at the time. It could be pouring, storming, raining, a blizzard, or whatever, and she would never let him spend the night. He had to get out of that house. We would even say, "Well momma, it's too bad out there, don't let him go out like that." She'd never let a man stay there with her and her girls overnight. We knew her boyfriend very well, but never once did she let him spend a night. My mother never let it happen. If I were a single mother, I could never let a man spend the night.

ANONYMOUS

My mother and father split up when I was thirteen. My mother always told me, "That is your father and nobody can stop you from having a relationship with him." So one year we were with our mom and the next we were with our daddy. We would switch back over, keep switching back and forth. I always said that when I grew up, I wanted my baby's daddy to be there with me all the time, not this switching back and forth. When I got pregnant, my baby's daddy told me it wasn't his baby. At first I felt like I couldn't live without her having a daddy. I cried my whole nine months of pregnancy. So now I know that I don't need no baby's daddy to love my baby. I will love her because she is here and can't nobody take that away from me.

HARRIET AND LONNIE

"There is no man in this whole world who will take care of all your needs, so get yourself something you can do to take care of yourself." My mom, especially meant for us to be financially independent. She would say that even if you get married and your husband has a good job, he could divorce you, get sick or disabled and you need something to fall back on to take care of yourself and your future. She also said, he can't be responsible for making you happy, "Be happy yourself and other things will follow."

JANICE AND VERMA

My mother often says two things that put problems into perspective. First is that when life hands you problems, put your problems in God's hands. Secondly, she says don't let problems get you down, let them remind you to look up. I've found this advice to be helpful during those times when I just can't figure out what to do about something. My mother is facing cancer right now and we have put this in God's hands. I keep looking up and she keeps getting better.

DAISY AND JESSIE

She felt like women have the power to control and that we should be in control at all times because we were smarter. I was taught that you did not have to give up yourself to maintain relationships. The best way to maintain a relationship is not to give. The more you don't give, the more you can get out of a man. She talked a lot about what you can get out of a man without giving up anything. My mother shared with me that she never really did love my father. She sort of raised me to believe that women don't have to love their men. They're just there with them, for the convenience of it. Even though I was married for fifteen years, I don't think I was really in love with that man. A whole lot had to do with the messages that my mother sent. Learning from that first experience, I chose out of love this time. I'm sure it's love and a lot of the input that my mother had always shared me with as far as him being a good provider.

ANONYMOUS

Well, my mother always said, "You got to stop letting people destroy your dignity and self-worth. You got to keep on living no matter what. If you're with someone who doesn't want to move forward and love you for you, let him go, shrug your shoulders, and considerate it their lost. You're too beautiful for the bull." I've heard this from her a million times. Did I listen? Heck no! So now I'm learning the hard way right now that my mother was and IS always right. After all, she's been through it already. My daughter is only eight-years-old, but I'm already teaching her to stay away from those negative folks. I have already embedded in her brain, school before babies, school before babies, school before babies. I told her once she gets her degree, she could do whatever she pleases. She's already a straight A student and I'm going to make sure it stays that way.

DORRETTA AND DORIS

I can remember as a child, being upset that my father wasn't paying child support. She would say that she would never send him to jail for not paying child support. She said, "You are his kids and he can decide whether he is going to support you or not. I would like for him to support you, but if he doesn't, you don't have to worry. You will be supported but it will be his loss." He would come over and if we needed money we would call him. But that was her, to be bigger. So now, I tell my friends, if he isn't going to pay, that's his issue. He is going to lose in the end. You have enough money to take care of your kids without spending all this money and energy in court with this man who has decided to divorce his kids too. It's his loss and he's the one who will have to try to make it up later on. I definitely got that from her.

VICKY

My mother is now seventy-eight years old. She has always been very youthful. It makes me very sad because my mother is a person who doesn't want to get old. That's because her personal identity is tied to how she looks, her persona. She had this great figure, this dangerous walk, that other women didn't want their husbands' around. This is also a woman who was very much into clothes and fashion. She lost her figure. She is not sexy like she used to be. The problem is that she still wants to perceive herself the way she was. It's all tied up in how she looks. She's had a very difficult time.

HELEN AND PEARL

The most interesting thing about my mother's change of life is that she was always so full of life and so vibrant. Then all of a sudden one day I went to visit her and she was an older woman. It was like, when this happen? I don't remember the gradual changes, it's like it was overnight. It got so bad that it became very difficult for me to accept it. Her personality changed, as well as her desire to live life in the full and spirited way that I had grown to take for granted. It seemed as though she decided one day that she was old and she was going to start acting old. She was going to start looking old and there was nothing that we could do to change that. I can remember so clearly saying, "So you don't like your long hair anymore. Let's go out and get your hair cut into a cute little cut. It's salt and pepper, and it's real curly, and it will look really pretty." She said, "No, I just want to wear it in a little ball and then put on a wig." It was like, well I'm a grandma now. It was pretty traumatic, pretty scary, and quite abrupt. I didn't handle it very well. I really backed off, I know I did. I thought it was a temporary state of being and she just never came back.

143

Then one day she really was old, so you have to start accepting the reality of the health problems and the restrictions, and you just go with the flow. My husband tells me I am getting just like her. It's food for thought. It really is.

SANDI AND EVA

This will be my first Mother's Day without the physical presence of my mother. And while she is not physically present on this earth, her Spirit dwells and exists in another world. These past few months have been a process of grieving, releasing, surrendering, accepting, and healing. There are daily reminders of her unconditional love, compassion, creativity and generosity. The heartache and heartbreak is being mended, healed and restored with all the wonderful memories. The memories that at first brought tears and sadness are now bringing joy, gratitude and acknowledgement of the gifts and blessings of birth, nurturing, love, support, comfort, inspiration, wisdom, encourage-ment, and the guidance to the magnificent and unconditional love of God. The memories are reminders that we are always loved, that we are never alone, and that everything, and I do mean everything, is always in Divine Order.

CLAUDETTE AND MARIA

My mother is seventy-nine years old. She's very active and she gets around. There's no mistake about it. She looks twenty years younger and has got more energy than any of us. Age has definitely not slowed her down, not by any means. She thinks she's going to live forever. Of all eight of us, I think it would be interesting to see who would end up being her primary caregiver. I know a home would definitely not be an option for her. But we have not approached that.

JUDY AND SYLVIA

When I asked her how she handles life's ups and downs so smoothly, she responded, "You must learn not to become upset or distressed by things that are beyond your control." She also sets an example by her own loving ways. She always has time to listen or to do, is eternally patient, and gives uncondi-tional love, always.

BRENDA

I think of this mother figure often. I will never forget those wonderful words of wisdom that she passed on to me almost thirty years ago, after I had done something really, really stupid. Those words have carried me through many a thunderstorm, life's storms. I have shared those words with my little ones. She said, "You will look at this situation in years to come and you will realize that there will be bigger challenges to deal with. This will pass and you will get over it." Those words have carried me through many trials and they are so true. I thank you! My children have come back to me many times and said, "You know mom, you were right."

MICHELE AND BOBBI

You may get tired, digging, digging, digging and looking for the treasure. But remember the person who dug day after day and finally gave up, threw the shovel down and walked away in disgust. Another person seeing this frustration came to look at this hole and out of curiosity picked up the shovel and dug into the same dirt and with one blow found the treasure. Don't give up too soon.

HELEN AND PEARL

My mother taught me that there was no time to be down and out. There was no room for disappointment. You can't really afford to be disappointed. You do what you need to do and you keep pushing along. My mother is a remarkable woman. I am oftentimes in awe around what she did in a lifetime raising the children and doing what I consider to be a very effective job. She provided the time, attention, and the caring for her kids while living up to the demands of a very forceful husband who did not tolerate anything less than perfection. I thought she just did a tremendous job. She was a very strong woman, very tough all around, and she passed that on to all of her daughters.

BENNA AND MARY

She always said, "Whenever you are trying to attain something, if the door is locked, try the window. If you can't get in, open the roof. If that's not possible tunnel underneath. Get There."

HELEN AND HELEN

On perseverance. "Don't worry about it if that didn't work. There is more than one way to skin a cat." As simple and childish as this may sound, it has always worked for me. I don't give up. I just find another way.

LENA AND TERESA

Never leave your house a mess. You never know how you may have to come back. You may get sick while out and someone may have to bring you home. Then they will see how you live. Even if you aren't a dirty person, if your house is a mess that one time, that's what they will think about.

KIMBERLY AND MARY

"I saw it when it drove up." These words of wisdom aided me in my growth and allowed me to "see" some of the things that she "saw." I have also heeded these words so that I would not make unnecessary mistakes.

SERENA AND PEARL

For a woman who never worked, my mother kept some money of her own. She'd hide money and when I needed special things, she'd go to the linen closet. Carefully hidden between towels and sheets, she'd pull out money tightly wrapped in a handkerchief. This was her "stash." I was raised to believe that a woman should always have a "stash," some money that the man would not know about.

ANITRA AND HAZEL

My mother never talked much, and I never understood her until I became an adult. The things I learned from her were through example. I do remember her saying, "You've got to take care of yourself." I used to think that it meant to learn to support yourself. Now that she is a double amputee with diabetes, I now get what she meant. You've got to put you first.

MARY LOU AND MARY LOU

I was named after my mother so that makes me a junior, the second, or a namesake. One of the best things my mother did for me (besides giving birth to me) is taught me how to be resilient and non-judgmental in one statement. Anytime some "drama" occurred because of my own or other people's foolishness, she would say to me, "Just think of this as a learning experience." She never criticized, condemned, or judged me. She only loves me for who I am and who I strive to be. What more can you ask from any one person?

ANITRA AND VIOLA

The second thing she taught me was to make an entrance. My grandmother was the "pillar of the community" type, and when she entered the room, all eyes were always on her and what she planned to do.

CONNIE AND DAISY

My mother taught me to live my life regardless of my possessions. I recently read an article on the value of love and relationships versus the value of possessions. I often wondered how my mother could be satisfied without having many things that other people had. As I grew older, I learned to appreciate life and be grateful to God for the things I do have. Unfortunately, we only see each other once a year and no matter how old I am, I still miss my mom.

CASSANDRA AND ROSE

My mother was letting me know that beauty is within and in your attitude. One day she looked up to me and said, "You're a pretty girl, but you are ugly because you have nasty ways." I am very careful the way I treat people. Also, I know that when people see me, they see natural beauty and are waiting to see the way that I act.

CAROLYN AND JESSIE

On Faith and Expectation: When you pray (asking God for anything), you can immediately look for and receive your answer because, "God always answers." Jessie has, and still lives by this now, for almost one hundred years. It doesn't matter what the prayer is, she looks for the answer(s) immediately. I remember having a headache one time and she called me over to her. She said a prayer and when she was done, she looked at me and asked, "How's your head now?" I told her it still ached. She said, "It will be gone in a minute because when I ask God for something, God always grants me." Of course, in a matter of moments, my headache was gone and I have lived by that example (there are many more) all of my life.

CIE AND MAUREEN

One of many things that I remember my mother sharing with me when I was too young to appreciate it is, "The Bible teaches us to be as wise as serpents and gentle as lambs." Many years later, God led me to this passage in the Bible, but I remember it most as my mother's words. They have guided me through difficult situations, usually involving difficult people. Just recently, I had the pleasure of reminding my mother of "her" words as I tried to persuade her to take a healthy stand against an injustice in her life. Life is indeed circular.

PAULA AND HATTIE

"You can't make chicken salad out of chicken sh__!" Her recipe comes in handy when one is dealt a bad hand of cards at bid, or on any other occasion when a sister can't get the job done because she hasn't got the right tools.

SHARON AND ANNELLE

In a difficult period of my life my mother said that once your' know a person's Spirit and determine that their Spirit means you no harm, they can never again hurt you because you now know what you need to do to change yourself.

JILL AND ALLENE

"Let every pot sit on its own bottom." She meant that everyone should pull his or her own weight. She also implied that we were all in the same situation. We may be adorned differently, but in the end, our "bottoms" are alike.

ARLENE AND NANA

"Life will offer you either lessons or blessings." If you look at your experiences in this way, you can create a win-win outlook. If you learn from an experience, you have benefited from it.

ODESSA AND NAOMI

Whenever there was some sort of upheaval in our lives, my mother always used to tell us, " Just be still." She meant that there are blessings that are coming but you'll get in the way if you keep going. You just have to be still. Once you put it out there you've got to be still. There are so many women trying so hard, and they are never still enough. They don't stop. I pass that on to my daughters. They always want things yesterday, but sometimes we have to stop and be still. I hear it in the air. When I feel myself getting too far out there, the words will just come out of nowhere. It seems to be good counsel for anybody. She would say, "This too will pass." However horrendous the pain, this too will pass. From her vantage point, the Lord made the decision. She did not like it, and it was clear that she wasn't happy, but it was to be lived with. Because life is life, and it's going to have these things in it.

YVONNE AND NAOMI

What is amazing to me sometimes, when I think about it, is that she was just our mom, but she was so smart and educated. She was so wise. She didn't finish high school. She always had the pearl. You needed a crutch she had a sentence or an expression. I'm the shortest thing in the family and I didn't like it and I was trying to grow forever and she would say, "Good things come in small packages." She was so great, and she was our mother. How really precious and wonderful that we had her and how terrible it is that she's gone. She was a beautiful woman, just a beautiful woman from the inside out. That's what she would say, "Beauty should be from the inside out."

DAISY AND JESSIE

She made it very clear when I was a teenager and in my early adult life, not to trust another woman, especially when it comes to your man. You're not supposed to tell your girlfriends about your personal married life or your personal affairs with your boyfriend, because a woman can't be trusted. They'll back stab you. They'll pretend to be your friend and try to get your man.

ODESSA AND NAOMI

I still feel my mother's Spirit around me. Everyday. Every single day. I never have a day where I feel alone. I haven't been to my mother's grave that often. I was standing there, not knowing what to say. You know, not wanting to cry and make her Spirit unhappy. I was in bad shape. I knew she knew what the real deal was, whatever it was. And the butterfly came. It came and just floated around and then it sat right down on my mother's grave, not my grandmother's or my grandfather's but on my mother's and stayed there. It didn't move. After that, every time I would come, the monarch butterfly would land on her grave ever so gently and just sit there. Mother used to talk about monarch butterflies. When we were there recently, putting in the new flowers, a monarch butterfly came and I said, "See that, there's the butterfly, that's her sign." I don't really understand. I've never taken the tact of doing research to read about monarch butterflies. I don't know that much about them. I just know it is the prettiest butterfly I've ever seen.

SERENA AND PEARL

I think at first, I was angry with her for getting old. Even though she is still young at heart, I initially missed her strength and energy. She started to complain about her health and her ailments, and I just couldn't understand it. I now understand that if she is to live, she must age. I think sometimes about loosing her, and I don't know if I could handle that. She keeps preparing me for that day. She has written up all the detail about how she wants her funeral, and that conversation upsets me. She tells me where she keeps this information and for the life of me, I just can't seem to remember. I just block it out.

RECLAIM YOUR STORY

Many of us have not taken the time and some of us have not had the opportunity to reflect with our Mothers about their lives as daughters. Too often, we allow our Mothers to walk and leave this planet, before we know about or understand the circumstances and experiences that make them the women that they are. We don't ask some of the basic questions about their lives, because, so frequently, we are seeking their guidance about our lives. Sometimes, we don't talk to them at all. We convince ourselves that their ideas, messages and wisdom are outmoded, old-fashioned and passé. We know them as our Mother, but we know far too little about them as daughters. We know even less about how their daughter experiences influence the women they become as our Mothers. All of their experiences help to shape who we are as daughters, and eventually, who we are as Mothers.

Use the questions that follow as tools to start a different conversation with your Mother or the Mother Figure in your life. These questions can begin as a reminiscence to help create a valuable understanding of who you are and who she is. Sharing the experiences of a lifetime through these questions and others you create, can draw you closer as daughter and Mother. Reclaim Your Story and the unique qualities that make you *This Mother's Daughter.*

RECLAIM YOUR STORY

What was life like for her while growing up?

What did she like to do?

Who were her friends and why?

Did she go to church? Where?

What kind of relationship did she have with her Mother?

What kinds of things did they do together? Argue about?

How was her childhood different from yours?

How did her Mother punish and reward her?

What was the worst thing she can remember doing as a child?
   How did her Mother respond?

 What is her happiest memory from childhood?

Where was she born?

What was her Mother's pregnancy like? The delivery? Was she breast fed?

Where did she attend school (elementary, high school, college)?

What kind of student was she? Did she complete her education?
   Why? Why not?

What subjects or activities did she enjoy in school?

Does she remember any special teachers? What was special about them?

Did she have any problems in school?

What did she want to be when she grew up? Did she do that and if not why?

What was her first job? How old was she?

When did she first start dating?

What was her first serious boyfriend's name? Why did she like him?

When and how did she first learn about becoming a woman?

What does she remember about the onset of her menstrual cycle?

What does she recall about her first sexual experience?

What did her Mother tell her about sex and sexuality?

What was her pregnancy and delivery like with you?

Did she breast-feed you? Why? Why not?

Has she ever been in love?

What did her Mother teach her about love? How does she define love?

How did she meet her first adult love? What were the attractions?

What does she think are the most important qualities to look for
   in choosing a partner?

What does it take to maintain a good relationship with your partner?

What types of partners does she seem to attract? Why?

What mistakes has she made in her relationships?

What changes has she seen in herself as she has grown older? Physical? Emotional?

How does she feel about growing older? Does she have any fears?

Where would she want to live if she became unable to care for herself?

Who is her best friend today and why?

Who has most impacted the direction her life has taken?

What traits does she have that her Mother had? Are these traits that she appreciates? Does she see any of these traits in you?

What were some of the most significant barriers or crises' she encountered in life and how did she overcome them?

How satisfied has she been with her life in general?

What would she do differently in life and in raising you if she could live life over?

Have there been any surprises, disappointments or unexpected pleasures in raising you?

What is the most important thing she has tried to teach you?

What particular wisdom did her Mother pass on that has helped in her life journey?

What particular message or wisdom does she want to pass on to you?

Are there cherished family or Mother/daughter traditions that she'd like to pass on?

Are there any secrets that she has kept that you should know about?

Does she think about her death? Does she have any preferences for her final arrangements?

CONTRIBUTORS OF
PEARLS OF WISDOM

Daughter	Mother	Daughter	Mother
Angela	Elaine	Barbara	Ann
Denise	Arrie	Barbara	Annie
Algata	Kate	Barbara	Geraldine
Amelia	Myrtle	Barbara	Magnolia
Amina Cora	Mary	Beahta	Royce
Angela	Carolyn	Benna	Mary
Angela	Elaine	Bernadette	Johnetta
Angela	Marie	Bessie	Anna
Angela	Tony Mae	Betty	Berniece
Ann	Annie	Betty	Sallie
Ann	Edith	Bettye	Ruby
Ann	Pauline	Beverly	Betty and Lois
Arema	Virginia	Beverely	Lorraine
Arlene	Nana	Brenda	Ann
Arlene	Ruth	Brenda	Carrie
Arnitra	Hazel	Brenda	Julie
Arnitra	Viola	Brenda	Maxine
Axe Maia	Johnnie	Candace	Margarete
Barbara	Elizabeth	Carla	Geneva
Barbara	Juanita	Carolyne	Jessie

DAUGHTER	MOTHER	DAUGHTER	MOTHER
Carolyne	Lillian	DeVora	Hazel
Carrie	Eddie	Diana	Bertha
Cassandra	Rose	Dominique	Linda
Cassandra	Margaret	Donna Lynn	Ruth Deloris
Celia	Barbara	Doris	Irma
Charmaine	Christine	Dorretta	Doris
Cherronda	Mary	Dovetta	Olivia
Cherronda	Ivory	Edith	Pearl
Cheryl	Frances	Edwyna	Elgertha
Christine	Dorothy	Elaine	Sylvia
Cie	Maureen	Elinor	Gina
Colette	Alice	Ena	Georgiana
Conni	Daisy	Essie	Annie
Cynthia	Wilma	Esther	Annie
Cynthia	Esther	Eula Belle	Amlilian
Cynthia	Olevia	Eunice	Edith
Cynthia	Carolyn	Evelyn	Lela
Dana	Darlene	Evelyn	Vernice
Deborah	Alice	Faye	Vivian
Deborah	Ruth	Felicia	LaVera
Debra	Naomi	Feranda	Warner
Debra	Lenora	Gail	Elinor
Dee	Ceal	Gail	Estella
Delores	Kathleen	Genise	Lillie Mae

DAUGHTER	MOTHER	DAUGHTER	MOTHER
Geraldine	Elsie	Joe Ann	Helen
Gloria Bennett	Rachel	Joy	Alberta
Gwendolyn	Virginia	Joyce	Corine
Gwen	Rosetts	Joyce	Bertha
Harriette	Lonnie	Joyce	Eloise
Hattie	Nancy	Juanita	Elsie
Helen	Helen	Judith	Sue
Helena	Dolla	June	Hilda
Helene	Maxine	Karen	Lillian
Helene	Norma	Karen	Fannie
Ida B.	Leotha	Kimberly	Vivian
Ida	Jeannette	Kimberly	Mary
Imani	Josephine	Kimberly	Affeteen
Iris	Iris	Kristin	Sharon
Irment	Mattie	Lena	Maria
Jacqueline	Charlotte	Lenora	Mackie
Jaella	Dorothy	Leshia	Bernice
Janay	Yvette	Lillie	Danella
Janis	Elizabeth	Linda	Bernice
Jean	Magnolia	Linda	Loretta
Jeanette	Addie May	Linda	Lula
Jeanne	Mary Louise	Linda	Ophelia
Jill	Allene	Linda	Ruth
Joann	Irma	Lisa	Debra

DAUGHTER	MOTHER	DAUGHTER	MOTHER
Lonnetta	Augusta	Otelia	Bettie
Loretta	Doris	Pamela	Theda
Lori	Margaret	Pat	Dorothy
Mable	Ruth	Pat	Mary
Mae	Annie	Patrice	Shirley
Mae	Eula	Patricia	Nadine
Margaret	Mamie	Patricia	Laura
Mariana	Anna	Patricia	Marie
Marsha	Ruth	Paula	Hattie
Martha	Lelia	Pepper	Ruth
Marvia	Mavis	Regina	Cherry
Mary	Eunice	Renae Jeanene	Earline Joyce
Mary	Mary	Renee	Dorothy
Mary	Emma	Renita	Opreabea
Mary	Joanne	Rena	Anna
Mary	Linda	Rev. Brenda	Sylvia
Maxine	Elvie	Rev. Leona	Minnie
Michele	Bertha	Rikki	Marie
Michelle	Bobbie	Robin	Rose
Natalie	Alice	Robin	Olive
Natalie	Evelyn	Rodneye	Marie
Nelvia	Daisy	Rolanda	Carol
Nichell	Celia	Rosalie	Evelyn
Olenter	Della	Rosamond	R. Marie

DAUGHTER	MOTHER	DAUGHTER	MOTHER
Rose	Jennie	Stephanie	Arnita
Ruth	Edna Mae	Stephanie	Charlotte
Ruth	Naomi	Suzette	Hattie
Sadie	Kizzie	Sylvia	Lillie
Sammella	Luella	Tiffany	Rev. Princella
Sandi	Eva	Tiffany	Denise
Sandra	Flora	Tina	Louise
Sharisse	Juliene	Tomi	Alice
Sharon	Olivia	Verma	Bertha
Sharon	Vivian	Victoria	Rosa
Sharon	Annelle	Vilma	Ella
Sharon	Deloris	Viretha	Annie
Sharon	Olivia	Wendy Delnise	Johnnie Mae
Sheila	Frances	Wynona	Lucy
Sheila	Rutha	Wynona	Ruby
Shelley	Joyce	Yolanda	Addie Lee
Sheridan	Helen	Yvette	Sharon
Shunielle	Gail	Yvonne	Ethel
Shyvonne	Sharon		
Sonja	Roxie		

Notes

Notes

_____

_____

_____

_____

_____

_____

_____

_____

_____

_____

_____

_____

_____

Notes

Notes